Product Tankers

First published in 2016 by
Nick Tolerton & Merivale Press

ISBN 978-1877418-23-5

Pre-press work by transpressnz.com, Wellington

Printed by Prolong Press, China

Ship's particulars in the captions in this book list the following data (where it is known): Ship's name, owner, manager, flag, builder, year of completion, deadweight tonnage, length overall, number of tanks, cranes or derricks and their safe working load, engine and capacity, service speed, and photo credit.

Vessel dimensions in this book are given in metrics. For readers interested, the overall lengths of representative product tankers in Imperial measurement are:

War-built T2 type — 159.5m = 523ft 3in
Shell 1950s H class — 169.4m = 555ft 9in
BP 1960s Bird class — 160 m = 524ft 11in
Typical 1970s product tanker — 170 m = 557ft 8in
Modern 47,000dwt Hyundai standard design — 183.2 m = 601ft
Modern LR2 110,000dwt product tanker — 244 m = 800ft 6in

Half-title: *Torea* in heavy weather (Warren Nelson)

Titlepage photo: Troodos Shipping's *Cyprus Glory*, ex-*Andrea Brovig*, from Shin Yamamoto, 1975. (Nick Tolerton).

Front endpaper: The *Jane S* of 2015 from Hyundai Mipo. (Chris Howell).

Back endpaper: A famous name revived — the *Pamir* of 2004 from Hyundai Mipo. (Trevor Jones).

Chkalov **– USSR-Georgian Shipping Co, USSR; Kherson Shipyard, Kherson, 1956; 11,915 dwt, 145.5 m, 24 ta, 1 ho, 1x5 tn der, 2 x Russkiy-Skoda 4000 bhp, 12.5kn. (Trevor Jones)**

Representatives of two large tanker classes from the USSR: The 11,915 dwt product tanker *Chkalov* (above) of 1956 from the Kherson Shipyard in the Crimea was one of about 50 twin-engined, single screw motor-ships of this type built in the 1950s and early 1960s. These *Kostroma* class ships, allegedly based on the U.S. T2s, were the the mainstay of the Soviet tanker fleet at this time. The 5045 dwt oil and vegetable oil carrier *Ayon* (below) of 1969 was one of about 40 similar vessels commissioned by the Soviet Union from Finnish shipbuilder Rauma-Repola.

Ayon **– USSR-Primorski Shipping Co, USSR; Rauma-Repola, Rauma, 1969; 5045 dwt, 106.15 m, 10 ta, 1 ho, 1 x 2 tn der, 2900 bhp Valmet-B&W, 14kn. (Tolerton)**

Texaco Oslo – Texaco Norway A/S, Norway; Blythswood Shipbuilding, Glasgow, 1960; 20,034 deadweight, 174.91 metres; 30 tanks, 8800 bhp Rowan-Doxford, 14.5 knots. (Trevor Jones)

What a difference 30 years makes: the classic tanker *Texaco Oslo* of 1960, pictured above on the New Waterway in 1984, and the modern chemical-products carrier *Gulf Moon* of 2007, also photographed on the Waterway 30 years later, reflect how tankers have evolved. The former was a product of Blythswood in the heyday of British shipbuilding, and the latter one of a large number of similar ships from today's kings of product tanker construction, Hyundai Mipo.

Gulf Moon – Gulf Moon Shipping Ltd (Gulf Energy Maritime), Bahamas; Hyundai Mipo, Ulsan, 2007; 37,488 dwt, 184 m, 12 ta & 2 slop ta, 10,686 bhp Hyundai-MAN-B&W, 14 kn. (Anton de Krieger)

Product Tankers

Nick Tolerton and Michael Pryce

STI Notting Hill – STI Notting Hill Shipping Co (Claus-Peter Offen Tankschiffreederei), Marshall Islands; Hyundai Mipo, Ulsan, 2015; approx 51,840 dwt, 184 m. (Anton de Krieger)

Once the huge fleets of the oil majors and state-owned oil companies dominated the carriage of products. Today the big players are companies like Scorpio Tankers and Navig8 which have gone on construction sprees after successfully wooing sharemarket investors. Two of the latest ships in their fleets are *STI Notting Hill* (above) and *Navig8 Almandine* (below), both 2015 completions from Hyundai Mipo. The *Almandine* was the first in a series of 18 ECO chemical-oil tankers for Navig8 from Hyundai Mipo.

Navig8 Almandine – Navig8 Chemical 1 Tankers Inc, Marshall Islands; Hyundai Mipo, Ulsan, 2015; approx 37,596 dwt, 184 m. (Anton de Krieger)

Contents

Mikom Brave – Mikom Transport Pte Ltd (MMS Co.), Singapore; Shin Kurushima Dockyard, Onishi, 2000; 45,869 dwt, 179.88 m, 12,600 hp Kobe Hatsudoki-Mitsubishi, 14.6 kn. (Captain Peter Stacey, above, and Nick Tolerton, below)

Two angles on a typical product tanker trading today, *Mikom Brave* — a deck view taken in Wellington harbour (above) and pictured under way (below) in the colours of Japan's NYK Lines. Built by Shin Kurushima Dockyard in 2000, this 45,869 dwt vessel was sold in 2008 to become *Faneromeni A.*

Introduction

Oil tankers were easily noticed in past times by having their engines and funnels aft, so were always prominent by being different in a shipping world that was comprised mainly of cargo liners and tramps with their engines in the middle. After the giant Anglo-Iranian (BP) refinery in Abadan was nationalised in 1951, the nations that consumed the oil looked to review how they supplied their markets, and switched from "source-refineries" (one of which had just been nationalised!) to new refineries built in the country which was using the finished product, hence Shellhaven, Isle of Grain and other refineries sprang-up in Europe and the Far East — much safer!

However, this resulted in the tanker trade starting to focus on the transport of large quantities of crude oil from foreign oilfields, and such ships, usually carrying just one grade of crude oil, could be built much larger. Thus was born the age of the super tanker, with ever-increasing sizes reaching (and passing) 65,000 tons dwt, 100,000 tons dwt, 150,000 tons dwt, 200,000 tons dwt etc, each new "largest tanker" being graphically described in the world's media.

During the 1960s and 1970s, most new ships adopted the same design as tankers, with engines and accommodation aft. At the same time, most tankers dispensed with their 'midships accommodation and moved that aft as well, so it became more difficult to pick out the tankers from bulk carriers, which all looked similar in the distance.

While the media spotlight was focussed on the latest "biggest and best," a quiet revolution was also taking place in the smaller tankers that were built to carry refined oil products around the coasts of consumer countries – the product tankers. They could not be as large as the crude-carrying super-tankers, as they needed to be able to use the smaller ports built near centres of population. The size of their cargo parcels was much less – usually nobody wanted 200,000 tonnes of petrol in one delivery! So while their big sisters hogged the limelight, the product tankers quietly evolved as a specialist ship, becoming more efficient, all motor ships, and gradually getting larger and becoming more standardised. By the 1990s, the oil companies had ceased having tankers specially designed and built for them, and they gradually adopted shipyard standard types of about 45,000 tons dwt for ownership or charter.

This book tells the story of the development of product tankers, their builders, classes, owners, and trades. It covers the early days of general purpose tankers (which could carry 'black' or 'white' products), to specialist tankers carrying only white products, and onto product-chemical tankers, which again can usually carry black or white products again. Most of these tankers did not receive wide publicity, and probably went largely unnoticed outside the oil industry, but they play a vital role in quietly delivering the lifeblood of the modern world.

Ohio Sun **– Sun Oil Co., USA; Sun Shipbuilding & Dry Dock Co., Chester, Pennsylvania, 1943; 16,772 dwt, 159.5 m, 7240 shp steam turbine & Westinghouse 6000 shp electric motor. (Trevor Jones)**

Appearing almost as built, the *Ohio Sun* was built as *Kenesaw Mountain*, one of many T2 tankers from the Sun Shipbuilding & Dry Dock Co in Chester, Pennsylvania. Like many Sun completions she took her name from a Civil War battle, although curiously Kennesaw is normally spelt with two n's. Renamed in 1948, she survived collision with the German heavy lift ship *Wartenfels* in the Houston Ship Channel in 1961 and stranding in a hurricane off Sombrero Key, Florida, in 1964 before going to shipbreakers in Kaohsiung in 1969.

than to commit capital to an entirely new ship for ventures that at that time seemed fraught with many uncertainties. The most famous, perhaps, of these conversions was *Ideal X*, a 1945 T2-SE-A1 completion from Marinship as *Potrero Hills*. Converted by Bethlehem Steel, Baltimore, to carry containers on a spardeck, she made the pioneer service sailing for Malcolm McLean, the father of container shipping, with 58 containers from Port Newark to Houston in 1956.

Other dramatic cannibalisations saw T2s modified to operate as floating space tracking stations for NASA for the Apollo moon project (three of the "Mission" A2s), as pioneer chemical and gas tankers, self-discharging colliers, lightering tankers, grain storage vessels, and suction dredgers. Several were also converted for use in Norway and later by the US military during the Vietnam War as floating power generation stations, utilising the turbo-electric machinery and the cargo tank capacity for fuel oil for the boilers.

One of the most intriguing transmogrifications was the Kaiser-built *Oregon Trail* of 1943, renamed *Herman F Whiton* in 1948, and bought a year later by Aristotle Onassis. He had the T2 rebuilt at Howaldtswerke, Kiel, into a whaling factory ship, *Olympic Challenger*, flagged in Panama. Onassis's pirate venture was highly lucrative, but outrageously flouted the then fairly feeble international whaling regulations. The conversion included a stern ramp and four large funnels in pairs, making her totally unrecognisable as a T2. The whaling voyages from 1950 to 1956 saw the Onassis fleet arrested in November 1954 for breaching Peru's claimed 200-mile limit. The ship was sold to a Japanese whaling company in 1956 to become *Kyokuyo Maru No. 2* and went to Korea for demolition in 1975.

One of the last T2 survivors in largely original condition was USS *Saugatuck*, an A1 type from Sun, launched as *Newtown* in 1942, which after navy service was laid up in the James River, Virginia, reserve fleet until 2006 when she was put up for disposal and, in spite of her obvious heritage values, apparently broken up locally.

The last T2, the 1944 Marinship A2 completion *Mission Santa Ynez* went to shipbreakers in Brownsville, Texas, in 2010 after being laid up in the Suisun Bay reserve fleet from 1975. Tankers may lack the glamour of passenger ships, classic sail vessels, and warships, but it is a small tragedy that no T2 was preserved.

In addition to the T2 types, more than 60 tankers were built in United States shipyards to a modification of the famous Liberty ship dry cargo design.

The wartime construction of standard tanker designs was not confined to the United States. At British shipyards production embraced three main Empire ship classes. Thirty-four 12,000 dwt tankers, some of them motorships and some of them triple expansion steamers, were built from 1941 to 1945 as the Ocean-type ships — also known as the "Three 12s" because of their deadweight and their fuel consumption of 12 tons a day at 12 knots. Based on a Shell design, construction was spread around seven shipyards, and 22 survived the war to go into commercial service.

Another 21 Empire tankers, also with a mix of oil and triple expansion steam machinery, were built from 1941 to 1945 to the 14,500 dwt Norwegian-type design, based on the Westfal-Larsen sisters *Sandanger* and *Eidanger* of 1938 from Sir James Laing & Sons. These 21 were built by Furness Shipbuilding, Haverton Hill (six), and Laing, Sunderland (15). Only two were lost during the war.

An improved class of thirteen 15 kn, 11,900 dwt Standard Fast steam turbine tankers was built 1944-46 also mainly by Furness Shipbuilding and Laing. Fast ships for their day, they did not need convoy escort. All survived the war and were taken after it by the Admiralty as fleet auxiliaries.

Although only a relatively small number were lost during the war probably because of their speed and improved convoy techniques by the time they came into service, the T2s had their share of mishaps in peacetime.

One of the most unfortunate and one with an extraordinary history even among the many convoluted tales of the T2s was *Fort Mercer* of 1945 from Sun Shipbuilding. She broke in two in a severe storm off Cape Cod carrying a cargo of fuel oil and kerosene from Norco, Louisiana, to Portland, Maine, on February 18, 1952, with the loss of five lives. Remarkably, another T2, *Pendleton*, a 1944 Kaiser completion, on passage New Orleans-Boston with kerosene and heating oil, broke in two nearby on the same day in the same storm, the doubleheader disaster reviving concerns about the strength of welded hulls and a recommendation for additional crack arrestors to be fitted to T2 hulls. The stern section of *Fort Mercer* was salvaged with nearly half her cargo intact, and the bow section was sunk by the Coast Guard. A new fore section was constructed by Todd Shipyards, Houston, and she returned to service under the US flag as *San Jacinto* in 1953 for the Trinidad Corporation of New York. On March 26, 1964, still owned by the Trinidad Corporation she broke in two again (pictured) after an explosion off Chincoteague, Virginia, while sailing from Portland, Maine, to Jacksonville. Both sections were salvaged and spawned two ships — the stern being joined with a new fore and midship section to create the 190 m tanker *Pasadena*, and the fore and cargo sections of the *San Jacinto* with the aft section of another T2, *Mission San Carlos*, plus the installation of two 45 tn cranes, to create the 16 kn container and rail car carrier *Seatrain Maryland*, one of seven similar T2 hybrid container conversions for Seatrain. Both 'new' ships went on to give many more years service — although presumably their crews would have been a little nervous if Portland was ever a port of call. The *Seatrain Maryland* went to Kaohsiung in 1985 to be broken up; the history of *Pasadena* ended at Chittagong in 1983.

Cannon Beach – **War Shipping Administration, US; Kaiser Co., Portland, 1945; 16,572 dwt, 159.56m, 26 ta, 7240 shp steam turbine & General Electric electric motor, 14.5 kn.**

A fine example of a T2 in wartime-rig — *Cannon Beach*, a 1945 T2-SE-A1 completion from Kaiser's Portland yard, photographed early in 1946 still with her wartime guntubs and quick release Carley floats. In the post-war disposal of the T2s, she was sold in 1948 and traded without change of name for the Panama Transoceanic Co, one of the many American-owned T2s under the flag of Panama. The ship was given a new fore-body and midship section at Hamburg in 1960 (increasing her deadweight tonnage to 23,580) and renamed *Carolyn E Conway*, eventually going to breakers in Brazil in 1975.

Beecher Island – **British Tanker Co., UK; Alabama DD, Mobile, 1944; 16,495 dwt, 159.56 m. (World Ship Society)**

T2s were useful acquisitions for BP and Shell after the war. BP took 10, and all retained their rather evocative names. *Beecher Island* (above) and *Rogue River* (below) were both 1944 completions from Alabama Dry Dock & Shipbuilding purchased in 1947, and in the fleet until 1959. That year the former went to Barrow for demolition while *Rogue River* was sold to Norwegian owners to be used as a floating power generating plant in Sweden before being lengthened with a new forebody and converted into a bulk carrier in 1961. She finally went to Kaohsiung for demolition in 1977.

Rogue River – **British Tanker Co., UK; Alabama DD, Mobile, 1944; 16,494 dwt, 159.56m (World Ship Society)**

Cottonwood Creek – **British Tanker Co., UK; Alabama DD, Mobile, 1944; 16,505 dwt, 159.56 m. (World Ship Society)**

Cottonwood Creek (above) was another 1944 Alabama completion. She was transferred to a French BP subsidiary in 1955 and renamed *Brissac*, then sold in 1959 to be converted into a bulk carrier, renamed *Bulk Mariner.* Given the name *Cottonwood Creek* again in 1960, she broke up after grounding on the coast of Honduras in January 1970 while sailing from New Orleans to Saigon with bulk wheat and bagged rice. She was American-owned and flagged at that time.

Shell took 19 T2s in 1947, and all were given names beginning with 'T.' Typical of them was *Theodoxus* (below), built by Kaiser as *Modoc Point.* All but one were broken up in the UK, and *Theodoxus* followed a familiar path out of the fleet for these ships, going to Faslane in 1962.

Theodoxus – **Shell Petroleum Co., UK; Kaiser, Portland, 1945; 16,568 dwt, 159.56 m.**
(Shell Fleet Association)

San Leonardo – **Eagle Oil & Shipping Co., UK; Kaiser, Portland, 1944; 16,500 dwt, 159.5 m. (World Ship Society/Keith Byass**)

Eagle Oil and Shipping Co. of London acquired two T2s, *San Leonardo,* above, built as *Bryce Canyon*, and *San Leopoldo* (ex-*Laurel Hill*), below. Both were 1944 completions from Kaiser Co. at Portland and came to Eagle in 1949 after brief service with Shell as *Turbinellus* and *Tresus* respectively. Both went to Scottish shipbreakers in 1961. Now a forgotten company, Eagle Oil once had one of the most important tanker fleets. It ordered no less than 19 new ships after being formed in 1912 to carry oil from Mexico, with one of them, *San Fraterno* (1913/16,000 dwt), the world's largest tanker at the time. In World War Two its *San Demetrio* (1938/12,132 dwt) made an epic escape from the pocket battleship *Admiral Scheer*. Shell took over Eagle in 1959, and in 1964 Shell names replaced the evocative "San" names and the dramatic Eagle funnel also disappeared.

San Leopoldo – **Eagle Oil & Shipping Co., UK; Kaiser, Portland, 1944; 16,500 dwt, 159.5 m. (World Ship Society**)

Esso Glasgow – Esso Petroleum Co., UK; Sun SB & DD Co, Chester, 1944; 16,143 dwt, 159.56 m, 26 ta.
(World Ship Society/Keith Byass)

Esso took nine T2s for service in its UK fleet including *Esso Glasgow* of 1944 (above), built by Sun as *Wauhatchie*, and given a new 94 m midbody in 1957 to carry different grades of fuel in the British coastal distribution runs. In 1967 she was badly damaged by twin explosions and fire while berthed at Fawley (below), but returned to service. Esso's last T2, she went to shipbreakers at Bilbao in 1971.

Stanmore – Stanhope SS Co. (J.A. Billmeir & Co.), UK; Sun SB, Chester, 1945; 16,586 dwt, 159.5 m. (World Ship Society/Keith Byass)

Long-gone London tramp shipowner Jack Billmeir and his Stanhope Steamship Co. are best remembered for running supplies to the Republican forces during the Spanish civil war. After World War Two the company operated two T2s bought in 1947, including *Stanmore* (above) — astonishingly, Billmeir's seventh ship of that name even though his company was only established in the early 1930s. Built by Sun as *Fort Jupiter*, she was broken up at Faslane in 1960. She was employed in the mid-50s shuttling crude on the 12-hour run from Lake Maracaibo to Esso's Aruba refinery until a scrape on the bar meant repairs at a Brooklyn dockyard and a welcome three-week break in New York for the crew. *Performance* of 1943 (below) from Alabama, looking extremely smart although the photo was taken within a year or so of her going to shipbreakers in Kaohsiung in 1975, was built as *Little Big Horn*. Conspicuous in both photos are the original wartime bridges with portholes which must have afforded rather constricted visibility.

Performance – Summit Industrial Corporation, Panama; Alabama DD, Mobile, 1943; 17,019 dwt, 159.57 m, 27 ta. (Don Brown/Trevor Jones collection)

H.D.Collier **– Standard Oil Co. of California, US; Sun SB, Chester, 1945; 16,520 dwt, 159.5 m. (World Ship Society/Keith Byass)**

Good examples of American flag T2s post-war are these two: *H.D. Collier* (above) and *Bull Run* (below). The last T2-SE-A1 built by Sun, *H.D. Collier* was completed for Standard Oil Co of California in late 1945, and gave her owner nearly 30 years service before going to shipbreakers in Kaohsiung in 1974. Also a Sun completion (one of the many with a Civil War name), *Bull Run* of 1943 had a much more convoluted career. It included commercial service for Mathiasen's Tanker Industries of Philadelphia (in whose colours she is pictured), lay-ups in the reserve fleet, service for the US Navy in 1956-57 as USNS *Bull Run*, and con-version in 1969 to a containership for Sea-Land Service using the aft section of *Bull Run* and mid and fore sections of the C4 cargo ship *Anchorage* (ex-*Marine Panther*). The 'new' ship was named *Anchorage*. She was scrapped at Brownsville, Texas, in 1980.

Bull Run **-- Mathiasen's Tanker Industries, US; Sun SB, Chester, 1943; 16,730 dwt, 159.5 m. (World Ship Society/Keith Byass)**

Chevron Leiden -- Chevron Tankers (Nederland) NV, Netherlands; Alabama DD, Mobile, 1944, & Hitachi SB, Kawasaki, 1966; 22,762dwt, 172.3 m, 18 ta, 4x2 tn der, 7240 shp stm turb & 6000 shp General Electric electric motor, 14.5 kn. (Nick Tolerton)

Chevron Leiden (above) was one of the T2s so extensively rebuilt as to be unrecognisable from what she was originally. Completed by Alabama Dry Dock as *Fort Ridgely* in 1944 and renamed *Caltex Leiden* (Dutch flag) in 1950, she went to Hitachi, Kawasaki, in 1966 to have new 18-tank cargo and bow sections fitted. The stern superstructure was also rebuilt with, obviously, a new funnel, although it looks as though her original bridge was also incorporated in this. Renamed *Chevron Leiden* in 1968, she was damaged by a turbine explosion late in 1976 and towed to Kaohsiung early the next year for demolition. Another Alabama completion as *Boonesborough* of 1945, *Chevron The Hague* (below) received identical surgery from Hitachi in 1967, but lasted until 1983 when she arrived at Santander for demolition. It's unlikely that any of today's product tankers will sail nearly 40 years.

Chevron The Hague -- Chevron Tankers (Nederland) NV, Netherlands; Alabama DD, Mobile, 1945, & Hitachi, Kawasaki, 1967; 22,352 dwt, 172.4m, 18ta, 2x5 tn 2x3 tn 2x0.5 tn der, 7240 shp stm turb & 6000 shp GE electric motor. (Nick Tolerton)

Chevron Venice — Overseas Tankship Corp, Panama; Alabama DD, Mobile, 1945, & Hitachi, Innoshima, 1965; 24,029 dwt, 170.69 m, 18 ta, 2x2 tn der, 7240 shp stm turb & 5930 shp GE electric motor. (Nick Tolerton)

Chevron Venice (above), another Alabama completion as *Cabusto* of 1945, received less severe surgery. As *Caltex Venice* she went to Hitachi's Innoshima yard in 1965 for new forward and cargo sections. However, she retained her 'three island" configuration, although apparently with some modification to the stern house including a new funnel and hances. She gained a Chevron name in 1968, and in 1977 arrived at Kaohsiung to be broken up. Another tanker to retain that basic configuration but still transformed from the ship which slid down the ways at Sun Shipbuilding in 1944 was Texaco's *Texaco London*. Built as *Esso Utica,* she was rebuilt and lengthened at the Blythswood yard, Glasgow, in 1961 for Texaco. She was sold by Texaco in 1976 and scrapped at Brownsville the following year after a stranding.

Texaco London – Texaco Panama Inc, Liberia; Sun, Chester, 1944, & Blythswood, Glasgow, 1961; 24,498 dwt, 175.19 m, 27 ta, 2x5 tn 2x3 tn der, 7420 shp stm turb & 6600 shp Westinghouse electric motor, 14.5 kn. (World Ship Society/Keith Byass)

Texaco Bombay – Texaco Overseas Tankship, UK; Sun, Chester, 1945 & Hitachi, Kawasaki, 1968; 23,708 dwt, 167.49 m, 18 ta, 2x2 tn der, 7240 shp stm turb & 6000 shp Westinghouse elec motor, 13.5kn. (Don Brown/Trevor Jones collection)

A dozen Texaco/Caltex T2s were jumboised mainly in the 1960s. It involved a spectacular transmogrification for several operated by Texaco's British flag subsidiary Texaco Overseas Tankship, including these two, *Texaco Bombay* (above) and *Texaco Rome* (below), which were lengthened, widened, and deepened with new cargo sections and bows at Hitachi Zosen's Kawasaki yard in 1968. The traditional catwalk seems to have been dispensed with, too. The former was built as *Castle's Woods* by Sun Shipbuilding and the latter as *Sideling Hill* by Alabama Dry Dock. Both had Caltex prefixes to their names until 1968, when they were reconstructed, and, as the illustrations show, hardly looked war-built ships after that. *Rome*, which was disabled with alternator damage on a voyage Aruba-Curacao in October 1979, went to Kaohsiung in 1981 and her sister the following year – both further tributes to the longevity and adaptability of the T2s, and perhaps to Texaco's reputation as the thriftiest of oil's big 'Seven Sisters.'

Texaco Rome – Texaco Overseas Tankship, UK; Alabama DD, Mobile, 1945 & Hitachi, Kawasaki, 1968; 23,687 dwt, 172.40 m, 18 ta, 4x2 tn der, 7240 shp stm turb & 6000 shp GE electric motor, 14 kn. (Nick Tolerton)

Texaco Melbourne – Texaco Overseas Tankship, UK; Kaiser Co., Portland, 1945 & Hitachi, Kawasaki, 1967; 23,694 dwt, 172.40 m, 18 ta, 4x2 tn der, 7240 shp stm turb & 6000 shp GE elec motor, 13.25 kn. (World Ship Society/Keith Byass)

Similar conversions at Hitachi's Kawasaki shipyard in conjunction with a transfer to Texaco were also made for *Texaco Melbourne* (above) in 1967 and *Texaco Wellington* (below) in 1968. *Texaco Melbourne* was a Kaiser product, built as *Victory Loan* and becoming *Caltex Melbourne* in 1951. *Wellington* was built as *Paulus Hook* (named after the New Jersey community across the Hudson River from Manhattan) by Alabama in 1944 and took a Caltex name in 1952. The *Melbourne* sailed for 40 years before going to breakers at Porto Alegre in November 1985, while the career of the *Wellington* ended, like those of many other old tankers, at Kaohsiung in 1982.

Texaco Wellington – Texaco Overseas Tankship, UK; Alabama DD, Mobile, 1944 & Hitachi, Kawasaki, 1968; 23,680 dwt, 172.40 m, 18 ta, 4x2 tn der, 7240 shp stm turb & 6000 shp GE electric motor, 13.5 kn. (World Ship Society)

Marine Chemical Transporter – Marine Navigation Co., US; Kaiser Co., Portland, 1943; 16,014 dwt, 159.57 m, 26 ta, 7240 shp stm turb & 6000 shp GE electric motor. (World Ship Society/Keith Byass)

Polytimi Andreadis -- Stratis G. Andreadis, Greece; Sun SB, Chester, 1943 (aft section) & Hellenic, Skaramanga, 1963 (fwd & cargo sections); 25,184 dwt, 172.37 m, 4 ho, 7240 shp stm turb & 6000 shp Westinghouse electric motor. (WSS/Keith Byass)

The conversions the T2s were subjected to were varied and remarkable. A notable role for some was as pioneer chemical or gas carriers. *Marine Chemical Transporter* (top) was one example. She was completed as *Coquille* in 1943, and was rebuilt in 1955 to carry molten sulphur in two large insulated centre tanks, as well as chemicals in three stainless steel tanks. Others were converted to bulk carriers, like *Polytimi Andreadis* (centre), built as *Fort Niagara*, which was lengthened and converted in 1963. Owner Stratis G Andreadis, a Chiot, was an enormously influential if also sometimes controversial figure in the Greek shipping community and president of the Union of Greek Shipowners for 15 years from 1960. Greece was allocated only seven T2s in the postwar disposal of these vessels. Andreadis and six other owners bought one each for cash. A number of tankers were completed privately during the war for US companies, like *R.C.Stoner* (below), one of a trio for Standard Oil of California. Carrying aviation fuel from Honolulu, she foundered on a reef arriving at Wake Island in September 1967.

R.C. Stoner – Standard Oil Co of California, US; Sun SB, Chester, 1943, 17,870 dwt, 159.86 m, 2x GE stm turbs. (WSS/Keith Byass)

Lincoln – Federal Steam Navigation Co., UK; John Brown, Clydebank, 1958; 18,500 dwt, 170.07 m, 27 ta, 2 John Brown stm turbs 8250 shp, 14.5 kn. (World Ship Society)

Three more ships from the P&O programme were the steam tankers *Lincoln* (above) of 1958 and *Derby* and *Kent* of 1960, all from John Brown & Co. for Federal Steam Navigation. The latter pair of 48,800 dwt were crude oil tankers. *Lincoln*, sold in 1965 as *Amphion*, was broken up at Brownsville, Texas, in 1978 as *Phillips New Jersey.* She gobbled an alarming 50 tn of fuel a day – a motorship of comparable size like *Stonegate* (qv) consumed 28.

Pacific Star – Booth SS Co, UK; Wm Hamilton & Co, Port Glasgow, 1954; 16,700 dwt, 166.42 m, 27 ta, 6160 bhp Rowan-Doxford, 13 kn. (J. & M. Clarkson collection)

Even Blue Star and the Vestey family ventured into tanker shipping with the 16,700 dwt *Pacific Star* of 1954 from William Hamilton, Port Glasgow. She was registered at Glasgow in the ownership of Booth Steam Ship Co until 1961 when she was transferred to Blue Star Line, sold to Liberian owners as *Silver Bay* in 1964, and broken up in 1973 at Kaohsiung.

The Newcastle firm of Hunting & Son, established in 1874, was for many years the most prominent British independent in tanker shipping, completing its first tanker, the 5000 dwt *Duffield,* in 1893. By the end of 1908 it had taken delivery of six more. Its 15,760 dwt *Gretafield* of 1928 was one of the largest tankers of its day, and one of seven Hunting tankers to be lost in World War Two.

The distinctive Hunting funnel, black with narrow red and white bands and a blue star, was soon prominent again as the company rebuilt its fleet after the war to retain its preeminence among the UK independents. After acquiring several war-built standard designs, Hunting ordered 13 new tankers which were delivered from 1950 to 1959. Not surprisingly, most of them were ordered from northeastern shipbuilders, and they ranged from 12,442 to 32,160 dwt. Remarkably, none of them were sisters. One of the ships from this 1950s construction programme was the 16,800 dwt motor tanker *Avonfield* of 1953 (below), pictured in a lovely shot underway at Hobart. She was sold in 1965 and went to the breakers in 1973.

Hunting quit shipping in the early 1980s, and today is a PLC involved in specialist services to the oil and gas industries, and also in shipbroking.

Avonfield **– Eden Tankers (Hunting & Son), UK; Wm Doxford, Sunderland, 1953; 16,800 dwt, 163.98 m, 27 ta, 6450 bhp Doxford, 14 kn. (D.E. Kirby/R.A. Priest collection)**

Wheatfield **– Eden Tankers (Hunting & Son), UK; Furness SB, Haverton Hill, 1952; 16,500 dwt, 159.41 m, 5500 bhp Fairfield-Doxford, 14 kn. (World Ship Society)**

The second completion in Hunting's postwar construction programme was the 14kn 16,500dwt *Wheatfield* (above) of 1952 from Furness Shipbuilding's Haverton Hill yard. The 18,025 dwt *Teesfield* (below) of 1959, also from Furness, was the second to last. Eleven of the 13 ships, including both pictured on this page, were motor tankers. *Wheatfield* was sold in 1964 and broken up in 1976, and *Teesfield* farewelled the Hunting fleet to go direct to the breakers at Inverkeithing in 1978. She had operated at an economical 23.5 tn a day fuel consumption.

Teesfield **– Hunting (Eden) Tankers (Hunting & Son), UK; Furness SB, Haverton Hill, 1959, 18,025 dwt, 169.60 m, 27 ta, 6600 bhp Wallsend S&E-Doxford, 14 kn. (World Ship Society)**

As well as Hunting which was already well-established in the tanker trades, some other prominent north-eastern English shipping companies with long involvements in tramping expanded to tanker shipping in the 1950s. Turnbull Scott & Co. of Whitby and London and Ropner Shipping of Darlington both built tankers for charter, retaining management themselves.

Turnbull Scott's first was the steam tanker *Eastgate* of 1957 from J L Thompson, Sunderland, taken over as a Shell contract for one of the standard H class and bareboat chartered back to Shell for 20 years. She was followed in 1961 by *Stonegate* (below) from Smith's Dock, Middlesbrough. However, although also an 18,000 dwt general purpose tanker and likewise built on a 20-year bareboat charter to carry refined products for Shell, *Stonegate* was a motor ship, of a similar type to Shell's streamlined A class.

Vessels like *Stonegate* were an advance on the earlier general purpose tankers, able to carry more than one grade of oil. Demise-chartered tankers for Shell built to its H or K class designs were virtual sisters to Shell's own tankers with the same valves and internal pipeline systems to carry multigrade cargoes.

After two years in the clean oil trades, *Eastgate* worked in the dirty oil trades until 1966 when she was reverted to carrying white oils again. *Stonegate* was employed in the clean trades. Around 1965 both were employed trading from Shell's Rotterdam and Stanlow refineries to British, continental, and Scandinavian ports, and in 1966 on more hazardous work supplying South Vietnamese ports during the war. *Eastgate* was scrapped after serious collision damage off Hong Kong in 1973, and *Stonegate* was sold in 1981 as *Sunny* and arrived at Chittagong in 1985.

Stonegate **– Turnbull Scott Shipping Co., UK; Smith's Dock, Middlesbrough, 1961; 18,010 dwt, 170.30 m, 33 ta, 8000 bhp Hawthorn Leslie-Doxford, 14.5 kn. (R Wilson/R A Priest collection)**

Blyth Adventurer – **Blyth Dry Docks & Shipbuilding Co. (Moller Line), UK; Blyth DD&SB Co., Blyth, 1958; 18,825 dwt, 170.68 m, 30 ta, 9100 bhp Clark-Sulzer, 14 kn. (World Ship Society)**

Another prominent 'Anglo' Hong Kong shipowner was Moller & Co., which also bought the Blyth Dry Docks & Shipbuilding Co. in Northumberland after the Second World War and ran it until its closure in 1967. Among the completions at Blyth were the similar tankers *Blyth Adventurer* of 1958 (above) and *Hamilton Trader* of 1959 (below) for Moller companies. The well-named *Blyth Adventurer* was severely damaged while carrying naphtha in a grounding on the Horsburgh Shoal near Singapore in 1968, but was repaired and traded again before going to Kaohsiung shipbreakers 10 years later. The career of *Hamilton Trader* was also not without mishap. She is pictured below after a collision with the German coaster *Hannes Knuppel* in April 1969, when the tanker was anchored near the Bar Light Vessel in Liverpool Bay. However, like her fleet consort she was repaired and put back into service, sailing under another five names before ending her days at Chittagong in 1987.

Hamilton Trader – **Pacific Trading Co., UK; Blyth DD&SB Co., Blyth, 1959; 19,715 dwt, 170.68 m, 27 ta, 9100 bhp Clark-Sulzer, 14.5 kn. (Authors' collection)**

Norscot – **Norscot Shipping Co. (J. & J. Denholm), UK; C. Connell, Glasgow, 1953; 18.685 dwt, 169.46 m, 21 ta, 8500 bhp Barclay Curle-Doxford, 14.5 kn. (J.& M. Clarkson collection)**

Among the Scottish tramp companies, J. & J. Denholm showed notable initiative in the 1950s with expansion into tankers and ore carriers and joint ventures with other companies, notably Naess. It laid the foundation for Denholm, nicknamed the 'Glasgow Greeks,' to survive and thrive when its contemporaries disappeared. Its first tanker, the 18,685dwt *Norscot* of 1953 (above) from Charles Connell, Glasgow, was a typical general purpose motor tanker of the day. Chartered for seven years to Shell, she made an early voyage with petrol from the Pernis refinery, Rotterdam, to Fremantle-Albany-Adelaide, then carried a kerosene cargo from Freeport for Cochin-Madras-Calcutta, before switching to the black trades with crude oil from Mena al Ahmadi for Eastham. She was followed by the similar *Scotstoun* (below) from the same yard in 1956. With accommodation vastly superior to Denholm's tramps, the pair were popular ships with their crews.

Scotstoun – **Falkland Shipowners (J & J Denholm), UK; C Connell, Glasgow, 1956; 18,640 dwt, 169.46 m, 29 ta, 8500 bhp Barclay-Curle-Doxford, 14 kn. (J.& M. Clarkson collection)**

Baron Kilmarnock – Hogarth Shipping Co. & Kelvin Shipping Co. (H. Hogarth & Sons), UK; Caledon SB, Dundee, 1953; 16,875 dwt, 166.72 m, 6950 bhp Kincaid-B&W. (World Ship Society)

Another Scottish tramp owner, H. Hogarth & Sons, briefly tested the waters in the tanker trades with *Baron Kilmarnock* of 1953. Her austere lines are a contrast to the more flamboyant styling of some of her contemporaries illustrated in this chapter. A 16,875 dwt motorship from Caledon Shipbuilding, Dundee, she was Hogarth's first postwar newbuilding, but sold only four years later to the Bergen Line as *Spica*. Later owners converted her into a bulk carrier in 1966. Interestingly, Hogarth reverted to steam for a series of six 5400 gt tramps that followed *Baron Kilmarnock*.

Scottish Eagle – Scottish Tanker Co., UK; Swan Hunter, Newcastle, 1952; 15,710 dwt, 166.72 m, 20 ta, 6400 bhp Swan Hunter-Doxford, 13.5 kn. (Mike Pryce collection)

Before its 1955 merger with the Union-Castle Line which established the British & Commonwealth group, the Clan Line had also decided to dabble in tanker shipping. One of four tankers it operated in the 1950s through its Scottish Tanker Co. was the English-built *Scottish Eagle* of 1952 which went into service with a five-year BP charter, was sold to Pakistani owners 10 years later and sent for demolition in Karachi at the end of 1969. The Scottish Tanker Co. funnel differed from the famous black and red Clan funnel in having a narrow blue stripe between the two red bands.

Caltex Capetown – Seathrough Shipping Co., Greece; J. Boel & Fils, Tamise, 1958; 20,981 dwt, 170.69 m, 27 ta, 8600 bhp Cockerill-Ougree-B&W, 14 kn. (Trevor Jones)

Caltex was a joint marketing company for Standard Oil of California and Texaco, and two classic tankers which saw service in different parts of the world as 'coasters' for it were *Caltex Capetown* (above) and *Caltex Manchester* (below). A motorship built as *Eleftheroupolis* for a Papachristidis Liberian flag company by J. Boel in 1958, the former briefly became the Cypriot *Waikiwi Pioneer* in 1972 before taking her Caltex name in 1973 to distribute product to other South African ports from the refineries in Cape Town and Durban, under the Greek flag. *Caltex Manchester*, a steamship from Hawthorn Leslie, was chartered to operate on the Australian coast under Howard Smith management from 1964 to 1968. The *Manchester* was scrapped in 1972 and the *Capetown* in 1982.

Caltex Manchester – Overseas Tankship (UK), UK; Hawthorn Leslie, Hebburn, 1953; 17.510 dwt, 165.81 m, 27 ta, 2 Hawthorn Leslie s.turbs. 8200 shp, 14.5 kn. (World Ship Society)

Think oil tankers, think pollution. That seems to be the public perception, anyway. In Britain the *Torrey Canyon* disaster in 1967 kickstarted the environmental movement. Nearly 120,000 tons of crude oil spilled from this 118,285 dwt Liberian supertanker when she ran aground on the Seven Stones Reef bound for Milford Haven, and tankers and flags of convenience were in the spotlight again when another Liberian tanker, the 17,965 dwt *Dona Marika*, displaying the Chandris livery to less than advantage, was blown on to rocks at Milford Haven after anchoring in the roads in August 1973. She was carrying 5000 tons of petrol. About 3000 spilled, although the refined product was obviously less damaging than crude oil. Still looking a classic tanker even in these circumstances, *Dona Marika*, which was declared a constructive total loss after she was refloated in November, had been built as the Norwegian *Thorsorn* for Thor Dahl.

Dona Marika – Hermes Navegacion SA, Liberia; Kaldnes, Tonsberg, 1954; 17,965 dwt, 168.24 m, 6800 bhp Barclay Curle-Doxford. (Authors' collection)

One of the most fascinating aspects of the history of tanker shipping has been the prominence of the Scandinavian owners – particularly the enterprising Norwegians. That country's involvement in tankers dates to before World War One, when Wilh. Wilhelmsen took delivery of four tankers – the first to be wholly Norwegian-owned – starting with *San Joaquin* of 1913. Norway's first motor tanker (and the first tanker built with two longitudinal bulkheads), the 6800 dwt *Hamlet*, was completed by Gotaverken in 1916. From the tiny pre-war fleet, Norway's tanker fleet mushroomed to more than 2.1m dwt by 1939, by which time tankers made up 42% of the Norwegian merchant fleet. Norway could also boast the 2400 dwt *Moira* of 1935 from Swan Hunter as the world's first all-welded tanker. In the 1930s many tankers for Norway were built at Swedish yards on generous credit terms against long term charters with the oil majors.

Government restrictions on ordering vessels from overseas yards impeded Norwegian owners for a while after World War Two, but they eventually resumed their important standing in tanker shipping. Norwegian companies built up their fleets with a stream of orders for Swedish yards like Eriksbergs, Uddevallavarvet, Kockums, and Gotaverken, and British yards. At the end of 1955 Norway had the world's largest motor tanker fleet, 370 ships, and with 399 tankers in total trailed only Britain (537) and the USA (520).

Texaco Skandinavia **– Texaco Norway A/S, Norway; A/S Fredriksstad, Fredrikstad, 1962; 21,162 dwt, 176.33 m, 30 ta, 8750 bhp Gotaverken, 15 kn. (Tolerton)**

A classic Norwegian tanker, although this one operated for an oil major rather than the independent companies. *Texaco Skandinavia* was sold in 1986 and went to breakers at Alang in 1992. The highly raked bow was typical of tankers of her generation.

Polarprins – Hvalfangerselskap Polaris A/S (Melsom & Melsom), Norway; Barclay, Curle & Co., Glasgow, 1955; 18,377 dwt, 169.46 m, 27 ta, 1 ho, 3x5 tn 1x4 tn & 1x2 tn der, 8500 bhp Barclay Curle-Sulzer, 14.5 kn. (WSS/Keith Byass)

Some Norwegian owners with interests in whaling used their tankers to supply their Antarctic fleet with fuel oil and supplies in the season, chartering them out at other times of the year. One was Melsom & Melsom of Larvik, with *Polarprins* of 1955 (above) from Barclay, Curle typical of its vessels with their "Polar" names. The Melsom flourish of a white stripe on the hull was unusual in the utilitarian world of tankers. Another company with a whaling association was Svend Foyn Bruun of Tonsberg, whose small tanker fleet included the 19,706 dwt *Pepita* of 1957 (below) from Uddevallavarvet. *Polarprins* was broken up at Kaohsiung in 1974 and *Pepita*, sold in 1977, at Brindisi in 1988.

Pepita – A/S Pelagos (Svend Foyn Bruun), Norway; Uddevallavarvet, Uddevalla, 1957; 19,706 dwt, 170.72 m, 26 ta, 7x5 tn & 1x3 tn der, 7500 bhp Gotaverken, 14 kn. (Tolerton)

Haukanger – **Westfal-Larsen & Co. A/S, Norway; Burmeister & Wain, Copenhagen, 1958; 20,100 dwt, 170.68 m, 29 ta, 3x5 tn 1x3 tn & 1x1 tn der, 8750 bhp B&W, 15 kn. (M. Piche collection)**

Westfal-Larsen of Bergen has been prominent in both tanker and dry cargo shipping with a history going back to 1905, and before World War Two was Norway's biggest tanker owner with 12. Nine of them were lost in the war, but the company rebuilt its tanker fleet in the 50s with ships like the 1958 motor tanker *Haukanger* (above) from Burmeister & Wain. In 1976 she was sold to a Dannebrog company and converted at Singapore into the livestock carrier *Rosborg*, the bridge being moved to the bows to accommodate four tiers of steel pens to hold more than 30,000 sheep on export voyages from Australia. *Spinanger* (below) was another 1958 completion of similar size, from J.L .Thompson, Sunderland.

Spinanger – **Westfal-Larsen & Co. A/S, Norway; J L Thompson, Sunderland, 1958; 19,005 dwt, 170.38 m, 26 ta, 3x5 tn & 1x1 tn der, 8000 bhp Doxford, 14.5kn. (WSS/Keith Byass)**

Grenanger – **Westfal-Larsen & Co. A/S, Norway; Eriksbergs, Gothenburg, 1964; 19,980 dwt, 170.67 m, 35 ta, 2x7.5tn 3x5 tn 5x3 tn 4x1.5tn der, 8750 bhp Eriksbergs-B&W, 15 kn. (WSS/Keith Byass)**

Westfal-Larsen's 19,980 dwt, 15 kn motorships *Grenanger* (above) and *Austanger* of 1964 from Eriksbergs marked nearly the last hurrah for the classic three island with bridge amidships tanker. They contributed to the development of the WL and Odfjell chemical tanker fleet, but did not have stainless steel capacity. Both were sold to Vietnam Ocean Shipping Co. in 1975 for $10m as *Cuu Long I* and *Cuu Long II* respectively, and operated as clean product tankers for their new owners.

Fosna – **A/S J Ludwig Mowinckels Rederi, Norway; Smith's Dock, Middlesbrough, 1955; 16,400 dwt, 161.23 m, 27 ta, 5500 bhp Kincaid, 13 kn. (World Ship Society)**

J. Ludwig Mowinckels, established in 1894, was another Bergen company prominent in both liner and tanker shipping. Typical of its tankers in the postwar era was the 16,400 dwt motorship *Fosna* (above) of 1955 from Smith's Dock, which was sold in 1967 to become the Liberian *Eurochemist* and later traded under the Canadian flag as *Cabatern* and *Baffin Transport* before being towed in 1978 to Tuxpan, Mexico, for demolition.

One of the most successful independent product tanker operators has been Denmark's A.P. Moller. Best known of course as the giant of container shipping, Moller, founded in Svendborg in 1904, started in tankers with an investment in five new motorships in 1928 built for time charters to Shell and Standard Oil. They effectively paid for themselves within four years, and Moller has never looked back in the tanker business, expanding later of course to become the world's biggest container carrier as well as well as a major operator of giant VLCCs and gas tankers. It remains one of the major product tanker operators – and one of the few independent companies mentioned in this chapter which is still flourishing in the tanker business.

Brigantine – Brigantine Transport Corp, Liberia; Odense Staalskibsvaerft, Odense, 1949; 15,800dwt, 159.10m, 21ta, 4600bhp B&W, 13kn. (World Ship Society)

The 15,800dwt motor ship *Brigantine* was built at Moller's own Odense shipyard in 1949 for a French owner as *Floreal*. Almost a sister to several 1940s Maersk tankers beginning with *Henning Maersk* of 1940, she was purchased by Moller in 1956 to facilitate the Odense yard obtaining an order, sold in 1963, and converted to a bulk carrier 1964. Since she was not Danish-flagged, she was not given a Maersk name.

Alexander Maersk – A/S D/S Svendborg & D/S af 1912 A/S, Denmark; Mitsui, Tamano, 1959; 20,150 dwt, 170.38 m, 21 ta, 7900 bhp Mitsui-B&W, 15 kn. (World Ship Society)

Probably Moller's best-known class of product carriers in this era were the 20,000 dwt A class ships completed in 1957-59 which brought the distinctive Moller pale blue colours to ports worldwide. They included *Alexander Maersk* (above) and *Anders Maersk* (below). Six of them were built by Mitsui Zosen and a seventh by Hitachi Zosen, while the almost identical *Axel Maersk* was built in-house at Odense. A.P. Moller showed early initiative among European owners in ordering ships from Japan, and Mitsui had already completed a trio of cargo liners and the 18,645 dwt tanker *Gerd Maersk* for the Danish company as early as 1950, while *Adrian Maersk* of 1956 from Mitsui was a slightly shorter version of the As. All nine had seven centre tanks and 14 side tanks. By the end of 1960 more than 50 tankers had joined the Maersk fleet since the war. In 1965 the first 'modern' product tankers with coated tanks, the 5200 dwt *Dangulf Maersk* and *Svengulf Maersk*, both 5210 dwt and both built by Odense, carried the famous A.P. Moller seven-pointed star.

Anders Maersk – A/S D/S Svendborg & D/S af 1912 A/S, Denmark; Mitsui, Tamano, 1957; 20,115 dwt, 170.38 m, 21 ta, 2x7.5 tn & 2x5 tn der, 9200 bhp Mitsui-B&W, 15.5 kn. (World Ship Society)

Tuborg – R/A Dannebrog (Weco-Shipping I/S), Denmark; Hitachi Zosen, Osaka, 1965; 20,438 dwt, 170.69 m, 28 ta, 4x5 tn der, 7500 bhp Hitachi-B&W, 15 kn. (Tolerton)

The Danish tanker *Tuborg*, the fourth of five similar-sized ships completed 1956-66 by Hitachi for C.K. Hansen's Dannebrog, was of the last generation of classic three island tankers. With coated cargo tanks so she could also carry chemicals, she was an advanced product tanker for her day. *Tuborg* was sold in 1975 to Chilean owners as *Punta Angeles* for US $6.36 m — what one of the histories of Dannebrog gleefully describes as "almost unbelievably favourable terms." She went to Gadani Beach in 1997.

Taipieng – Nan Yang Shipping Co. (Ocean Tramping Co.), Somalia; Gotaverken, Gothenburg, 1950; 8962 dwt, 132.62 m, 24 ta, 4000 bhp Gotaverken, 13.5 kn. (Don Brown/Trevor Jones collection)

A 1950 completion for Haldor Virik of Sandefjord as *Sandefjord*, she was one of three small Norwegian tankers that were something of pioneers in the parcel trades, being fitted with separate pumps and lines to carry parcels of bulk lubricating oils. She became parcel operator Anco's *Anco Sailor* in 1964 before being taken over two years later by Ocean Tramping, China's Hong Kong-based shipping arm, and then becoming *Da Qing 402* in Mainland ownership in 1978. Her fate is uncertain.

Esso Yokohama – Esso Transport & Tanker Co., Panama; IHI, Kure, 1969; 21,445 dwt, 170.08 m, 27 ta, 7200 bhp IHI-Sulzer, 14.75 kn. (A. McMillan/R.A. Priest collection)

Esso Yokohama (above), another of the 1969 completions, was in the fleet until 1990, and after several changes of name went to Aliaga in 1995 for demolition. The pristine *Esso Bataan* (below) photographed at Island View, Durban, not long after completion in 1970, was transferred by Esso to its UK coastal fleet in 1983 as *Esso Tees*, and was sold in 1994 to be broken up at Alang.

Esso Bataan – Esso Tankers Inc, Liberia; IHI, Kure, 1970, 21,455 dwt, 170.08 m, 27 ta, 7200 bhp IHI-Sulzer, 14.75 kn. (Trevor Jones)

Messiniaki Anagennisis – Varkiza Compania Naviera SA (Michail A Karageorgis SA), Greece; Ishikawajima-Harima Heavy Industries, Aioi, 1970; 30,228dwt, 171.13m, 24ta, 1ho, 4x5tn & 2x3tn der, 11,200bhp IHI-Sulzer, 16kn. (above, Trevor Jones; below, Nick Tolerton)

The second ship of the IHI series for Michail Karageorgis was *Messiniaki Anagennisis* of 1970, shown leaving a South African port (above) and on the New Zealand coast (below). The goalpost mast forward was a feature of seven of the 18 ships. *Messiniaki Anagennisis* was sold in 1985 to become *Welcomer*, and after later trading as *Caliope* and the lamentably named *Puppy F* she went to Bangladesh in 2002 for demolition after an impressive career, for a hard working tanker, of more than 30 years.

Messiniaki Idea – Fortuna Oceanica Navegacion SA (Michail A Karageorgis SA), Greece; IHI, Aioi, 1972; 30,294 dwt, 171.13 m, 24 ta, 4x5 tn & 2x3 tn der, 11,550 bhp IHI-Sulzer. (Tolerton)

Messiniaki Idea (above) and *Messiniaki Lampsis* (below) were among the ones that did not have the goalpost mast, having an array of kingposts instead. Both were sold in 1984, with the *Idea* broken up in Turkey 10 years later, and the *Lampsis* going to Indian breakers a year earlier in 1993. Fuel consumption was about 37 tn a day.

Messiniaki Lampsis – Venus Ocean Corp (Michail A Karageorgis SA), Liberia; IHI, Aioi, 1972; 30,282 dwt, 170.72 m, 24 ta, 1 ho, 4x5 tn & 2x3 tn der, 11,550 bhp IHI-Sulzer, 16 kn. (Tolerton)

Alfios – **South Caribbean Shipping Co. (Sun Enterprises), Greece; Sumitomo HI Oppama yard, Yokosuka, 1983; 38,452 dwt, 171 m, 21 ta, 11,100 hp Sumitomo-Sulzer, 15 kn. (Tolerton)**

Two typical 1980s tankers, both with a Mobil connection: Both owned by a cheerfully named Greek company, South Caribbean Shipping Co., and completed in 1983, they are *Alfios* (above) and *Artemis* (below). The former, built as *Mobil Enterprise*, was one of a double hull trio for Mobil from Sumitomo, and the latter, originally *Mobil Courage*, which had a double bottom, was one of a large number of similar chemical-product carriers from Brodosplit.

Artemis – **South Caribbean Shipping Co. (Sun Enterprises), Greece; Brodogradiliste Split, Split, 1983; 39,776 dwt, 173.79 m, 26 ta, 11,400 hp '3 Maj'-Sulzer, 15 kn. (Tolerton)**

An Evolving Ship Type

The product tanker as a ship type blossomed in the 1970s and 1980s, with development taking a number of threads.

By now product carriers and crude oil tankers had evolved as quite separate ship types, the latter, of course, increasing enormously in size as 100,000 tonners and then much larger ships were built from the late 1960s onwards. However, it does not seem to be until 1968 that the term 'product' or 'products' carrier or tanker was first applied to designate the former. In the UK's industry bible *The Motor Ship*, the 5533 dwt Danish short sea trader *Esso Baltica*, described as "a product carrier which can carry up to four types of oil products, any three of which can be discharged simultaneously" may have been the first, in the June 1968 issue. Soon after came Cunard's "products carriers" *Lustrous* and *Luminous* (September 1968 issue) and the *Esso Bangkok* class "product carriers" (December 1968).

In 1982 *Fairplay* recorded the world product tanker fleet at 1586 vessels totaling 38.542 m dwt, more than half of them (810) owned by independent companies, with state operators including the USSR, China, Indonesia, Mexico, and several Middle Eastern nations operating 502 and the oil companies 274. Another 126 ships (3.54 m dwt) were on order.

The general purpose tanker of earlier days was now superseded by the purpose-built product tanker, and the typical vessel of the 1970s was a ship of 30,000 to 35,000 dwt, still with an overall length of about 170 m, necessary to access the older terminals built to cater to an earlier generation of tankers. Motor was by now the norm for product tanker propulsion, and after the oil shock of 1973 and its effect on bunker prices and improvements to engine design, motorships were almost universal in the tanker fleets even for the supertankers.

Many were flexible ships designed to operate in either the clean or dirty trades, and able to carry 10 or more grades of oils. Cargo pumping, piping, and stripping systems and tank coating, heating, and cleaning systems became more sophisticated. It became usual to fit heating coils to give vessels the flexibility to operate in the black oil trades even when vessels were primarily designed as clean product tankers. Cranes now sometimes replaced derricks for handling the hoses.

Owners looking at new tonnage — both crude and product tankers — also had to be mindful of increasing environmental concerns and the provisions of pollution prevention and safety legislation, notably MARPOL and SOLAS (reinforced by domestic legislation in some countries), mandating inert gas systems and segregated ballast tanks and restricting the discharge of slops.

Increasingly, there was an overlap between chemical and product carriage. The more expensive chemical tankers, with their larger number of tanks and more extensive cargo handling systems, frequently competed for clean product cargoes when conditions were difficult in their own specialty trades. And, more and more, owners primarily interested in a petroleum products carrier also wanted a vessel that could carry chemical cargoes, too.

By the end of the 1970s, owners were also frequently ordering vessels that were a new generation of the traditional general purpose tanker that could carry both clean products and black oils. It now meant the vessels being built with coated tanks for rapid cleaning for the transition from one type of cargo to the other between voyages, and heating coils for the black mode.

Another feature of this era was the advent of pools for smaller owners to combine their resources, which found particular favour among the many often relatively small Norwegian owners.

Although the largest product tankers of this era were smaller than today's giants, there was a growth in size among ships of this type, led to a large extent by Danish owner A.P. Moller, the largest independent operator.

The five ships of Moller's 55,000 dwt J class of 1974-78 from Kaldnes, Tonsberg, were the largest product tankers of their day, and designed for carrying both clean and black products — as well as crude trading if necessary. They were followed by six similarly flexible 64,900 dwt N class ships from Moller's own Odense yard which went into service in 1977-78, and five 50,000 dwt E class product tankers, also from Odense, in 1984-87. Five 55,000 dwt product tankers designed for black trades were built for Singapore-based Norse Management by Horten Verft, starting with the *Viking Gull* of 1979.

The United Kingdom also contributed some of the larger product tankers at this time. Harland & Wolff, Belfast, delivered the 66,600 dwt *Elstree Grange* and *Hornby Grange* to Alexander Shipping/Houlder Brothers in 1979, and Cammell-Laird completed seven tankers for the Vlasov group and the King Line (*Scottish Lion* of 1979 and *Scottish Eagle* of 1980) to its StaT 55 55,000 standard design in 1977-80.

The Jones Act vessels for United States domestic service are a separate thread, and the notable completion in this era was the 39,900 dwt *Chevron Oregon* of 1975 for the FMC Corporation of Portland. She was the first tanker built in the United States to be powered by a gas turbine, a 12,500 shp unit coupled to an electric motor, and was also notable for being of double hull construction.

Product tanker size took another jump early in the 1980s when the state-owned Kuwait Oil Tanker Co. introduced the 79,500 dwt *Umm Al Aish* and *Umm Al Maradem*, both completed in 1981 by Mitsubishi, Nagasaki, as well as three 65,000 tonners the following year. They were ordered when Middle Eastern oil exporting countries were looking in the 1970s to export a larger proportion of their production in refined form.

Another milestone in product tanker development came at the end of the decade when the Hadjieleftheriadis family's Eletson Corporation of Piraeus introduced a quartet of 46,538 dwt double-bottomed and double-sided product tankers. All built by Korea Shipbuilding, Busan, they were *Samothraki*, *Psara*, and *Halki* in 1989, followed by *Shinoussa* in 1990. All had six main tanks and four wing tanks.

A typical 1970s tanker profile – the Singapore-flag *VSP I* of 1975 (ex-*Maaskerk*). (Tolerton)

Texaco Rotterdam – **Tankship Finance UK Ltd (Texaco Overseas Tankship), UK; Wilton-Fijenoord, Schiedam, 1968; 24,062 dwt, 180.65 m, 22 ta, 2 x General Electric stm turbs 15,500 shp, 17.75 kn. (Tolerton)**

Almost the last hurrah for steam product tankers was a notable 24,000 dwt British-flag trio for Texaco, *Texaco Brussels* and *Texaco Ghent* from De Schelde, Flushing, and *Texaco Rotterdam* (above) from Wilton-Fijenoord, Schiedam, all completed in 1968. They were fast tankers with service speeds of 17.75-18 kn, their crews proud of their '500 club' in which all three had logged day's runs of more than 500 nautical miles. The trio could handle eight cargo segregations. A modern products motor tanker in service at the start of the 1970s was *Lustrous* of 1968 (below), built with her sister *Luminous* (1968) by Eriksbergs for the Cunard group, although her Moss Tankers livery hardly suggested a connection with the great liner company. She had two 12 cyl. Pielstick engines and a controllable pitch propeller, and publicity at the time of her introduction said the ship could maintain her service speed on one engine when sailing in ballast, and that *Lustrous* was one of the first deep sea tankers to use her main engines to generate power to drive the cargo pumps in port. The ship had 11 centre and 22 wing tanks, four electrically-driven centrifugal pumps, and a 6tn derrick and two 5tn derricks on the main deck, with a 1.5 tn derrick (stores) and a 5 tn derrick (for machinery parts and stores), both aft of the deckhouse. Fuel consumption was only 28 tn a day.

Lustrous – **Cunard SS Co. (Cunard-Brocklebank), UK; Eriksbergs, Gothenburg, 1968; 24,507 dwt, 169.63 m, 33 ta, 2 x Pielstick 10,080 bhp, 14.75 kn. (Tolerton)**

Contemporary with the Cunard pair were the 25,000 dwt *Laurelwood* (1969) and *Hollywood* (1970) from Doxford and Sunderland Shipbuilding, which could load or discharge eight different product cargoes simultaneously. They had 19 main cargo tanks, served by four steam turbine-powered pumps in the aft pumproom (each with an output of 700 tn an hour), plus four parcel tanks at the fore end of the cargo space, served by four steam pumps in the forward pumproom. Their appearance, with accommodation and bridge all aft, transom stern, and bulbous bow, has become fairly universal for product tankers.

Laurelwood – **John I. Jacobs & Co, UK; Doxford & Sunderland Shipbuilding, Sunderland, 1969; 25,200 dwt, 169.78 m, 22 ta, 2x10 tn & 2x2.5 tn der, 12,000 bhp Doxford, 15.5 kn. (plans, The Motor Ship; photo, Kingsley Barr/R.A. Priest collection)**

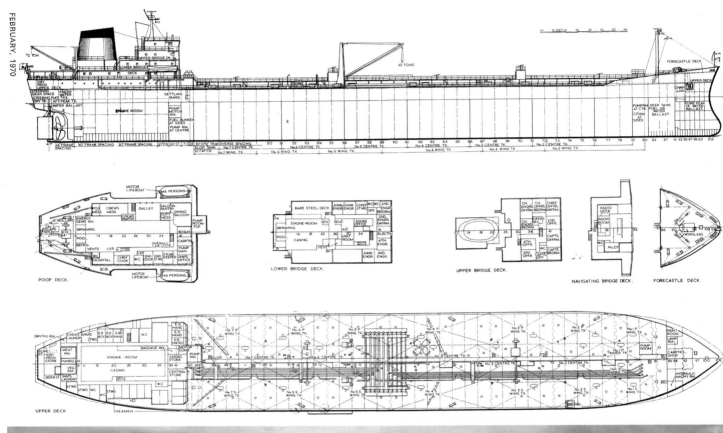

Asean Promoter – **Million Maritime Pte Ltd, Singapore; Horten Verft, Horten, 1975; 31,600 dwt, 168.76 m, 26 tk, 12,000 bhp Horten-Sulzer, 16 kn. (Tolerton)**

P&O through its Bulk Shipping Division gained two new product tankers with *Ardmay* and *Ardmore* – the latter pictured above when she was trading for Singapore owners later as *Asean Promoter*. Both were delivered in 1975 by the Norwegian yard Horten Verft. They were 31,600 dwt ships with 26 tanks and four pumps which could move 3000 tonnes an hour. Both were sold in 1983.

Clytoneus – **Blue Funnel Bulkships Ltd (Ocean Fleets), UK; Van der Giessen-de Norde, Krimpen, 1976; 56,050 dwt, 210.32 m, 21 ta, 2x10 tn der, 18,500 bhp B&W, 16.5 kn. (World Ship Society/Keith Byass)**

Blue Funnel Line also dabbled in tanker shipping in the 1970s in an ill-timed move that proved immensely costly during the group's sad decline. Two product tankers from Van der Giessen, the 56,050 dwt *Clytoneus* of 1976 and her sister *Cyclops* (1975), were at least not a drain on its finances like its supertankers and giant liquefied gas tanker *Nestor*. The famous blue funnel on *Clytoneus* was painted out in 1985 when she was sold to Singapore owners as *Affinity*.

No company was as industrious as Cammell Laird Shipbuilders in soliciting product tanker orders in the twilight of Britain's days as a major shipbuilding nation. A notable completion from the Birkenhead yard early in the 1970s was the 19,313 dwt *Esso Mersey* (1972) which was followed by the similar *Esso Clyde* (1972) and *Esso Severn* (1975), all built for Esso Petroleum Co. for British coastal distribution from Esso's refineries.

Esso Mersey could carry nine separate grades of clean oil products in 13 cargo tanks, served by four 750 hp electric cargo pumps, and also had two water ballast wing tanks. She was fitted with both bow and stern thrusters and a controllable pitch propeller, so could berth unaided. A novel feature of this tanker was high voltage electrical generating equipment for 3.3 kV power supply to the four cargo pump motors and the two thruster motors. She was designed to be manned by a complement of 28.

On the heels of completion of the first two Esso ships, Cammell Laird announced the introduction of two standard product tanker designs, the StaT 32 and StaT 50, to its portfolio. StaT stood for 'standard tanker,' and the company achieved mixed success with them. In 1973 John Hudson Fuel & Shipping placed a £20 m order for four 31,750 dwt tankers to the StaT 32 design, but financial difficulties prevented Hudson from taking delivery of these ships, which were eventually taken over by the Royal Fleet Auxiliary as fleet support tankers.

More fruitful was a £47 m order made later in 1973 for five 55,000 dwt ships for the larger design, now apparently scaled up as the StaT 55. Placed by the Vlasov group via Alva Shipping, the 55s were designed to be able to operate as black and clean oil carriers or as crude carriers. They had 21 epoxy-coated tanks.

The first of the Vlasov ships to be completed in what was the largest single order ever placed with Cammell Laird was *Algol* completed in 1976 and managed by Silver Line. When all were in service in 1980, they were operating as follows:

Algol time charter to Pemex, trading Mexico to US gulf.

Alkes time charter to Lagoven, trading Venezuela-Caribbean.

Almak time charter to Scandinavian Trading, trading trans-Atlantic.

Alvega time charter to Scandinavian Trading, trading Arabian Gulf-Aden.

Alvenus time charter to Maraven, trading North and South Americas.

Cammell Laird, part of British Shipbuilders from 1977, rounded off a productive decade in tanker construction with two more product carriers, the 56,000dwt sisters *Scottish Lion* (1979) and *Scottish Eagle* (1980) for British & Commonwealth's Scottish Tanker Co. *Scottish Lion* sailed from Falmouth on her maiden voyage in September 1979 on a charter for P&O Oil Trading to load gas oil at Sarroch (Sardinia) for discharge at Rotterdam, but soon after this was carrying non-heat crude oil cargoes from Puerto Bayovar to Los Angeles and from Esmeraldas, Ecuador, to Caribbean/US Gulf/US Atlantic coast ports. After trials at Falmouth and a naming ceremony there in March 1980, *Scottish Eagle* sailed for Flushing and loaded petrol, gas oil, and jet fuel for Lome, Togo.

Esso Severn – Esso Petroleum Co, UK; Cammell Laird, Birkenhead, 1975; 20,449 dwt, 166.50 m, 13 ta, 2x3 tn cr & 2x5 tn der, 2 x Crossley-Pielstick 10,920 bhp, 15.5 kn. (World Ship Society/Keith Byass)

The last of three twin-engined tankers from Cammell Laird, *Esso Severn* (above) served Esso in the British coastal trades until 1994 and was scrapped in China in 2000. They had 13 cargo tanks plus two water ballast wing tanks. Built to Cammell Laird's StaT 55 design for the British & Commonwealth group, *Scottish Eagle* and *Scottish Lion* (below) had 21 cargo tanks and an aft pumproom, with four steam turbine-driven cargo pumps. The tanks were epoxy-coated and fitted with aluminium brass heating coils, and both ships had Crude Oil Washing systems. The absence of a forecastle was a feature of this design.

Scottish Lion – King Line (Cayzer, Irvine Shipping), UK; Cammell Laird, Birkenhead, 1979; 56,490dwt, 210.01 m, 21 ta, 17,400 bhp Clark-Sulzer, 16.5 kn. (Trevor Jones)

The Canadian Pacific group diversified into tankers and bulk carriers in the 1960s through its Canadian Pacific (Bermuda) division, and after ordering four crude carriers it took delivery in 1973–76 of eight 30,000 dwt product tankers from Van der Giessen-de Noord, Krimpen. *G.A. Walker*, completed in 1973 and chartered to Esso, led the series and was followed by *W.A. Mather* and *R.A. Emerson* (named after CP executives) the same year. Then came five 'Fort' tankers – *Fort Macleod* and *Fort Steele* in 1974, the *Fort Edmonton* and *Fort Kipp* in 1975, and *Fort Coulonge* in 1976. With a fleet of 12 product tankers (four more 31,000 dwt 'Forts' were delivered from Sanoyasu Dockyard in 1980-81), CP ranked as the largest independent British operator in the early 1980s. The second of the Van der Giessen series, *W.A. Mather* was chartered to Shell for five years while under construction, and could carry four separate grades in 21 tanks served by four steam turbine-driven cargo pumps each with an output of 900 cu/m an hour. The tanks were coated in three coats of epoxy. She had a bulbous bow, now more or less standard on ships like this. Safety features in this class included fire-fighting foam nozzles on four platforms off the catwalk and a similar system in the cargo pumproom, a sprinkler system in the engineroom and pumproom, and fireproof alleyways in the accommodation. Ordered by CP when the company saw replacement potential in the aging world product fleet, the eight ships were all sold in 1988-89.

G.A. Walker – Canadian Pacific (Bermuda) Ltd, UK (Bermuda); Van der Giessen-de Noord, Krimpen, 1973; 30,607 dwt, 170.69 m, 21 ta, 12,200 bhp B&W, 15 kn. (K. Barr/R.A. Priest collection)

The lead ship of the class, *G.A. Walker* displays CP's idiosyncratic funnel marking to advantage in this photo at Hobart. She was sold in 1988 and went to shipbreakers in Chittagong in 2000 as *Alke*.

Mobil Endeavour – Mobil Shipping & Transportation Co., Liberia; Sumitomo HI, Oppama yard, Yokosuka, 1982; 33,187 dwt, 171 m, 21 ta, 11,100 bhp Sumitomo-Sulzer. (Tolerton)

Mobil went to Japan for a trio of 33,000 dwt ships which were completed by Sumitomo Heavy Industries in 1982-83 and Liberian-registered. With towering funnels and tall, sturdy kingposts for the hoses, they were dramatic looking tankers. Pictured above is *Mobil Endeavour* and below *Mobil Endurance*, the two 1982 completions. Cargo was moved by seven pumps of a total capacity of 3500 tn an hour.

Mobil Endurance – Mobil Shipping & Transportation Co., Liberia; Sumitomo HI, Oppama yard, Yokosuka, 1982; 33,235 dwt, 171 m, 21 ta, 11,100 bhp Sumitomo-Sulzer. (Tolerton)

Mercury – Scanmar Tanker Corp, Liberia; Eriksbergs, Gothenburg, 1974; 31,793 dwt, 170.77 m, 21 tk, 14,600 bhp Eriksbergs-B&W, 16.5 kn. (Tolerton)

It was becoming more and more difficult in the 1970s for West European shipbuilders to be competitive in the construction of vessels like tankers, with Swedish yards among those suffering most. *Mercury* (above) was a 1974 completion from Eriksbergs for the New York-based Maritime Overseas Corporation (later the Overseas Shipholding Group). She was a typical product tanker of this time, and the first of seven from Eriksbergs to this design. Five years later the yard completed its last ship, *Atland* for Brostroms – another of this class. Norway's smaller shipbuilding industry was also struggling to be competitive. *Texaco Baltic* (below) was a 1976 completion by Horten Verft and was followed by two sisters, *Texaco Bergen* and *Texaco Stockholm*, the following year. All three were built to operate for Texaco's Norwegian subsidiary. The satnav dome and deck crane were novelties on tankers then.

Texaco Baltic – Manufacturers Hanover Trust Co, Trustee (Texaco Norway A/S), Norway; Horten Verft, Horten, 1976; 31,502 dwt, 168.76 m, 24 ta, 12,000 bhp Horten-Sulzer, 16 kn. (Tolerton)

Panama – A/S Det Ostasiatiske Kompagni, Denmark; Nakskov Skibsvaerft, Nakskov, 1977; 33,401 dwt, 170.69 m, 24 ta, 12,500 bhp B&W, 15.25 kn. (Tolerton)

Denmark's venerable East Asiatic Co operated a small tanker fleet in the 1950s and 60s, and, diversifying like many cargo liner companies, returned to tankers with four vessels from its own Nakskov shipyard. *Patagonia* and *Pasadena*, both completed in 1976 for Eletson Maritime as *Piraeus Sea* and *Piraeus Sky*, were taken over after disagreement between the yard and the Greek owner, and the similar-sized *Panama* (above) and *Paranagua* (below) went into service in 1977. This quartet was followed by *Pattaya* from Nakskov in 1981. Later in the 80s EAC operated several more product tankers which were flagged out, and in 1990 took over three of Shell's F class product carriers before the famous EAC name disappeared from shipping near the end of the century.

Paranagua – A/S Det Ostasiatiske Kompagni, Denmark; Nakskov Skibsvaerft, Nakskov, 1977; 33,401 dwt, 170.69 m, 24 ta, 12,500 bhp B&W, 15.25 kn. (Tolerton)

State of the art in the mid-70s were four attractive 32,200dwt Belgian-flag tankers delivered to Nedlloyd subsidiary Ruys Bulk Transport, later Nedlloyd Bulk (Belgie) — *Maaskade*, *Maaskant*, and *Maaskerk* of 1975 and *Maaskroon* of 1976. Built by Boelwerf, Tamise, they were designed primarily as oil product carriers but, presaging tankers of the future, could also carry chemicals, type C in the main cargo tanks and type B in parcel tanks.

The hull was divided into 23 tanks, four of them smaller parcel tanks with stainless steel heating coils. The two aftermost wing tanks were fitted to be used as slop tanks. The hull had a double bottom through the centre tanks section.

These ships could carry 19 different grades and discharge four simultaneously from the main cargo tanks, while four separate grades could be carried in the parcel tanks. Two of these tanks had deepwell pumps, and there was a special pump for extremely viscous cargoes.

The main engine was a low-speed 13,500 bhp B&W, giving a service speed of 15.75 kn, and could be operated from the wheelhouse or the machinery control room. Other features included the cargo handling control room sited within the accommodation, and five firefighting monitors on raised platforms to cover the whole deck area. There were two 10 tn derricks for hose handling and two 4tn derricks aft for handling stern discharge hoses.

This quartet was followed by the similar-sized *Maassluis* and *Maasslot* of 1982 and *Maasstad* and *Maasstrom* of 1983, built by Van der Giessen and also designed for chemicals.

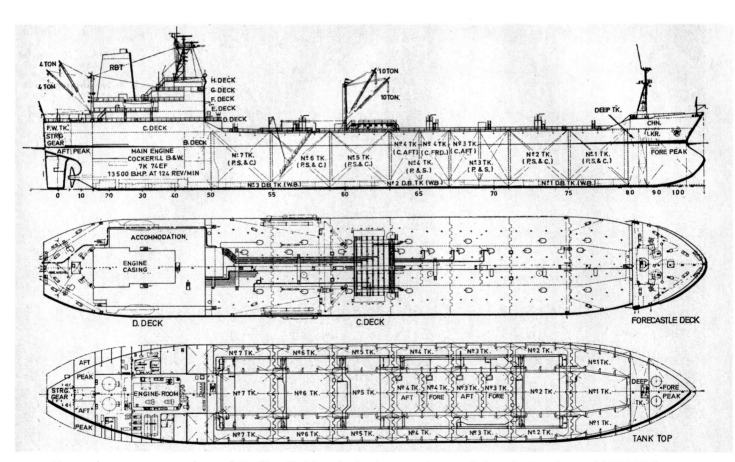

General arrangement plans of Nedlloyd's *Maaskade*-**class product and chemical tankers of 1975-76 from Boelwerf. (**The Motor Ship**)**

Maaskerk – **Nedlloyd Bulk (Belgie) SA, Belgium; Boelwerf, Tamise, 1975; 32,235 dwt, 170.69 m, 23 ta, 13,500 bhp Cockerill Ougree-B&W, 15.75 kn. (Tolerton)**

Third of the four product-chemical tankers for Nedlloyd from Boelwerf was *Maaskerk* (above) of 1975. Sold in 1985, *Maaskerk* was on the fifth name of her career when she traded for PP Petroleum of Singapore as *VSP I* (below), showing off her quite attractive lines to advantage as she speeds towards the Pulau Bukom refineries to load.

VSP I – **VSP Tankers Pte Ltd (PP Petroleum Pte), Singapore. (Tolerton)**

Better known for their supertankers, Greek owners have also of course been significant operators of product tankers. *Messiniaki Aigli* of 1969 mentioned in the last chapter is regarded as the first Greek products carrier, but was to be followed by many more, both new buildings and second-hand acquisitions, under several flags. Illustrated here are some of their tankers of the 1970s and 80s. *Marianna* of 1973 (below) and *Mando V* of 1972 were two sisters delivered to the Theodoracopulos' Metropolitan Shipping of Piraeus by Boelwerf, Tamise. A catwalk offset to starboard, an unusually long deck area aft, and two very large kingposts aft were features of these ships, and they had the by-now-standard bulbous bow. *Marianna* had 27 tanks served by four cargo pumps which could eject 3200 tn an hour. The engine was a 14,350 bhp Gotaverken and fuel consumption 45.5 tn a day. The Metropolitan Shipping pair was preceded by another ship of this type, *Tethys* (1972) for Tom Pappas' Atlantic Maritime Enterprises. *Marianna* was sold to Maltese owners in 1994 and broken up in India in 2003.

Marianna – Metropolitan Tankers (Metropolitan Shipping), Greece; Boelwerf, Tamise, 1973; 30,484 dwt, 173.54 m, 27 ta, 14,350 bhp Gotaverken, 16 kn. (Tolerton)

Taurus – Comanche Shipping Corp (Rethymnis & Kulukundis), Greece; Wartsila, Turku, 1977; 32,389 dwt, 171.35 m, 24 ta, 1x10 tn cr, 12,000 bhp Wartsila-Sulzer, 16.25 kn (Tolerton)

Michail Karageorgis added to its product tanker fleet in the late '70s with three 32,00dwt ships ordered from Wartsila, *Messiniaki Anatoli* and *Messiniaki Akti* of 1977 and *Messiniaki Avgi* of 1978, as well as taking delivery of a number of crude carriers around this time. However, Karageorgis quickly sold most of these ships, including *Anatoli* and *Akti* in 1979 and *Avgi* in 1980. *Messiniaki Akti* went to Comanche Shipping Corporation, one of London Greek owner Rethymnis & Kulukundis's companies, as *Taurus* (above). Sold again to Norwegian owners in 1988 and later to China, the ship went to Chinese shipbreakers in 2008. S Livanos (Hellas) took delivery of the sisters *Chios* and *Meandros* (below) in 1982 and *Evros* in 1984 from Mitsubishi, Nagasaki. A little extension to the forecastle was a feature of the trio. Three similar ships with Kriti names were delivered to another Greek owner, Avin International Corporation, by Mitsubishi in 1986. *Meandros* was sold in 1999 as *Creole* and broken up at Chittagong in 2007.

Meandros – Countess Shipping Co. (S Livanos), Greece; Mitsubishi, Nagasaki, 1982; 39,830 dwt, 178.01 m, 11 ta, 10,800 bhp Mitsubishi-Sulzer. (Tolerton)

The Niarchos-owned Hellenic Shipyards, Skaramanga, built a significant series of 31,000dwt product tankers beginning with five (four of them for Niarchos) in 1974-75, and then from 1982 another 10 to basically the same dimensions for the Soviet Union and the Niarchos group. The 1970s completions were *World Promise*, *World Prospect*, and *World Protector* (launched as *World Prospector*) of 1974 and *World Provider* and *Team Gerwi* of 1975. The lead ship *World Promise* had dimensions of 170.62 m (with a bulbous bow) x 26 m x 11 m. The 1980s completions for Niarchos were *World Process* and *World Produce* (1984), *World Prologue* (1985), and *World Prophet* and *World Prodigy* (1986), and they followed the Soviet orders *Dzerzhinsk*, *Novorossiysk* (launched as *World Product*), and *Stavropol* of 1982 and *Ulyanovsk* and *Urzhum* of 1983.

Aurora – **Master Shipping Co, Malta; Hellenic Shipyards, Skaramanga, 1983; 29,990 dwt, 170.69 m, 21 ta, 12,000 bhp Cegielski-B&W, 15.5 kn. (Tolerton)**

This anonymous and rather forlorn ship is the Valletta-registered *Aurora* about to be renamed *Marlina XV* for new Indonesian owners at Singapore in 2005. As the *Ulyanovsk* she was completed in 1983 as one of the Soviet quintet from Hellenic Shipyards. She had seven centre tanks and 14 wing tanks and four cargo pumps which could handle 3600 tn an hour. Later Cypriot-flagged, she was sold in 1999 and then traded as *Aurora* and *Marlina XV*. Her name was shortened to *Marlina* in 2011 and she was flagged in St Kitts & Nevis before she went, like so many of her generation of tankers, to shipbreakers in Chittagong that year.

World Promise – Medina Shipping Co. (International Maritime Agencies), Greece; Hellenic Shipyards, Skaramanga, 1974; 31,120 dwt, 170.62 m, 21 ta, 12,000 bhp Cegielski-Sulzer, 15 kn. (Tolerton)

Two of the 31,000 dwt series from Hellenic Shipyards: Like most of the series, the lead ship *World Promise* of 1974 (above) was built for shipyard owner Stavros Niarchos's own fleet. *Olympic Dream* (below) was the second and also completed in 1974 as *World Prospect*, but the next year, perhaps uniquely, went from Niarchos ownership to Onassis ownership. After sailing under eight different names, the former went to Indian shipbreakers in 2002 as *Pyrrihios*, while her sister was severely damaged in an explosion at Beirut in 1998 as the Maltese *Giovanna*, and went to Turkey in 2000 for demolition.

Olympic Dream – Moreno Shipping Co, Greece; Hellenic Shipyards, Skaramanga, 1974; 31,091 dwt, 170.75 m, 22 ta, 12,000 bhp Cegielski-Sulzer, 15 kn (Tolerton)

As well as these Greek-built tankers, several other notable classes of product tankers were built for the Soviet merchant fleet which expanded rapidly in the 1970s and 1980s. *Samotlor* of 1975 was the first of a series of 14 ice-strengthened tankers for Arctic service from Rauma-Repola, the last being delivered in 1978. These 17,200 dwt ships could carry crude as well as refined products, and had six centre tanks and 12 side tanks and a 950 cu/m dry cargo hold in the forecastle. The No.6 wing tanks both incorporated a small slop tank. A double bottom ran beneath the forecastle, tanks, and engineroom and the exterior side of the wing tanks was double-skinned. Ballast could be carried within the double bottom and double skin. Two 5 tn derricks were mounted on the goalpost mast forward which also incorporated an enclosed crow's nest, and there were also two 5 tn derricks for hose handling and a 3tn stores derrick. The pumproom was placed between cargo spaces and the engineroom, and cargo discharge was via four electric two-speed screw pumps.

Prominent among the Soviet Union's domestically-built product tankers was *Komandarm Fedko* series of nine 178 m, 27,400 dwt ships built 1976-1982 at the Kherson Shipyard, followed by a series of 11 slightly modified ships to this design completed 1983-88 by Kherson, starting with *Dmitriy Medvedyev*. Another 8 ships of this type were completed for Athenian Tankers in 1980-84.

Other notable product tanker classes for the USSR included 25 vessels of the 16,400 dwt *Josip Broz Tito*-type delivered from Yugoslav yards in 1984-89, 25 of the 22,000 dwt *Daugavpils*-type from Yugoslavia in 1965-71, 11 of the 40,000 dwt *Pablo Neruda*-type from Yugoslavia in 1975-79, seven of the 20,000 dwt *Internatsional*-type from Poland in 1968-70, and five 32,000 dwt ships from Swan Hunter Shipbuilders in 1975-77.

Rashleigh – Dezandis Co., Panama; Kherson Shipyard, Kherson, 1979; 27,360 dwt, 178.85 m, 16 ta, 10,600 bhp Bryansk-B&W, 15.25 kn. (Tolerton)

Pictured as *Rashleigh*, the name under which she went to shipbreakers at Alang in 2006, this ship was built as *Aleksandr Korneychuk*, one of 20 27,400 dwt ice-strengthened product tankers constructed at Kherson for the Soviet fleet in the 1970s and 80s.

Australian Pride – DMK Leasing A/S (A P Moller), Denmark; Odense, Lindo, 1987; 50,600 dwt, 182.02 m, 13 ta, 12,848 bhp Mitsui-B&W, 16 kn. (Tolerton)

Two of the 50,600 dwt class later became well-known ships in Australian ports. The last to be completed, *Oluf Maersk* (*Estelle Maersk* until 1992), was renamed *Australian Pride* in 1996 on charter for coastal service there and is seen above under that name. At the end of 2002 she and her sister *Olga Maersk* (see opposite) were purchased by BP Australia, registered to single-ship Singapore companies, flagged to the Bahamas, and put under ASP Ship Management with Australian crews. *Australian Pride* was renamed *Japonica* and *Olga Maersk* renamed *Jacaranda* (below). For the latter, this was accompanied by a large reduction in her measured deadweight for some reason.

Jacaranda – Perth Shipping Ltd (ASP Ship Management), Bahamas; Odense, Lindo, 1987; 44,997 dwt. (Tolerton)

In the mid-1980s Belgium's Exmar SA, Norway's Jahre Shipping, Naess Shipping of Bermuda, and Mitsui-OSK combined to set up PetroBulk Carriers, which introduced the innovative Cat class design from Boelwerf, Tamise, including *Petrobulk Panther* of 1985 (below), completed as *Naess Panther* and renamed the following year. PetroBulk's order for four Cat ships cost US$119 m.

On similar dimensions (171 m LOA, 32.24 m breadth, and 11.5 m draught) to a 30,000 dwt tanker, these ships offered 45,000 dwt and could carry a 48,500 cu/m petroleum cargo in up to 12 grades fully segregated. They also featured a double skin and double bottom, and an inverted deck structure, which, unusual though it looked then, has become fairly standard since. This meant the vessels did not require longitudinal bulkheads, and extra strength was achieved in the tanks through using corrugated transverse bulkheads.

With only eight main tanks/holds and three small tanks immediately aft of them, it required comprehensive tests and computer analysis by Boelwerf and the Delft University of Technology's ship hydromechanics lab, in collaboration with Lloyd's Register, to assess the sloshing risk in such large, undivided tanks when they were partially full.

The large tanks/holds were also intended to enable the ships to carry lighter dry bulk cargoes like grain, discharged pneumatically through small hatches. The eight main holds did not have wing tanks and were self-trimming.

For conventional tanker cargoes, the ships had 12 hydraulically-driven deepwell pumps which could discharge the cargo in 18 hours, cargo heating equipment on deck instead of internal coils, and crude oil washing, inert gas, and segregated ballast tanks. Speed was 14kn from a new design of low speed 11,150 bhp 4cy Sulzer engine from Cockerill.

Petrobulk Panther – **Petrobulk Carriers NV, Exmar NV, Esdam NV, & Boelwerf NV (Exmar NV), Belgium; Boelwerf, Tamise, 1985; 46,100 dwt, 171.81 m, 11 ta, 12 tn 5tn & 1 tn crs, 11,150 bhp Cockerill-Sulzer, 14 kn. (Tolerton)**

Lion – **Cortes Vessel Ltd Partnership (V Ships Norway A/S), Liberia; Boelwerf, Tamise, 1985; 46,100 dwt, 171.81 m, 11 ta, 11,149 bhp Cockerill-Sulzer, 14 kn. (Tolerton)**

Another of the Cat class (which grew to six ships) was *Jahre Lion*, also of 1985. She was renamed *Petrobulk Lion* the following year, and is pictured above under later ownership after being renamed simply *Lion* in 1996. PetroBulk was one of a number of pools set up for independent owners to combine their resources, and another of the initial vessels in its fleet was the smaller (in deadweight but not overall length), Japanese-built *Petrobulk Pilot* of 1985 (below), which also had COW, an inert gas system, and segregated ballast tanks. She had only seven tanks. *Petrobulk Pilot* was one of the neutral victims in the Iran-Iraq war, reportedly having two missiles fired at her by Iranian jets in February 1988 when she was outward bound in the Gulf with a cargo of petroleum products from Kuwait.

Petrobulk Pilot – **S.Y. Marine Co, Liberia; Onomichi Zosen, Onomichi, 1985; 39,008 dwt, 182.30 m, 7 ta, 9200 bhp Hitachi-Sulzer. (Tolerton)**

Lavender – Marubeni Maritime (Bermuda) Co. (Ajax Marine), UK; Kanda Zosensho, 1976; 32,769 dwt, 179.99 m, 13 ta, 12,000 bhp IHI-Sulzer, 15.75 kn. (Tolerton)

Japan dominated tanker construction in the 1970s and 80s, although product tankers tended to be the domain of its second-tier shipyards. A rather utilitarian-looking ship that is of interest for its port of registry was *Lavender* (above) completed by Kanda Zosensho in 1976 as *Ryuwa Maru* and renamed *Ginkgo* in 1978. In 1984 she became British owned as *Lavender* and registered, curiously for a vessel larger than a trawler, in Grimsby, operated by local company Ajax Marine. Even Norwegian owners were now shopping in Japan instead of Sweden – N.R. Bugge of Tonsberg operated *Kathy O* of 1981 from Hashihama Zosen and as *Pacific Current* (below) from 1984, registered in Liberia under both names.

Pacific Current – Pacific Current Inc (A/S N R Bugge), Liberia; Hashihama Zosen, Tadotsu, 1981; 37,271 dwt, 170.52 m, 11,700 bhp IHI-Pielstick, 14 kn. (Tolerton)

Stavanger Oak – K/S Stavanger Oak (Det Stavangerske Dampskibesselskab A/S), Norway; Hashihama, Tadotsu, 1981; 37,350 dwt, 170.52 m, 2 x IHI-Pielstick 11,700 bhp, 13.5 kn. (Tolerton)

Stavanger Oak was another 1981 completion from Hashihama of almost identical dimensions to *Pacific Current*, but differed in having two Pielstick engines. Built as *Seki Oak* for Japanese owners, the vessel was acquired in 1990 by the long established Stavanger company, Det Stavangerske Dampskibesselskab A/S (Stavanger Steamship Co), traditionally an operator of small coastal vessels, which built up a fleet of half a dozen product tankers around this time. *Fulmar* (below) of 1989 was one of several similar tankers from Onomichi. Built as *Kobe Spirit*, she became part of rising entrepreneur Stelios Haji-Ioannou's growing Stelmar Tankers fleet in 1993. The son of Loukas Haji-Ioannou who became the world's largest independent tanker operator as owner of Troodos Shipping, Sir Stelios was better known outside shipping for his easyJet airline, the flagship among several 'Easy' business ventures. *Fulmar* had only seven tanks and was probably essentially similar to *Petrobulk Pilot*, also from Onomichi.

Fulmar – Ariel Shipping Corp. (Stelmar Tankers (Management)), Greece; Onomichi Zosen, Onomichi, 39,521 dwt, 182.30 m, 7 ta, 9499 bhp Mitsui-B&W, 15.14 kn. (Tolerton)

Team Frosta was completed in 1981 as *Frosta* for prominent Norwegian owner J. Ludwig Mowinckels of Bergen and received her pool name the following year. She was built by Sanoyasu Dockyard, Mizushima, when European owners were increasingly switching to Japan for newbuilds, and was followed in 1982 by her sister *Troma*. She typified the trend towards product tankers designed to compete in the chemical trades (and, if necessary, even the crude), too, and as well as clean petroleum product cargoes she carried cargoes like molasses out of Mackay and Townsville, Queensland, while her sister brought a record cargo of caustic soda to Bunbury and Kwinana, Western Australia. *Team Frosta* was a 14.8 kn vessel of 41,985 dwt with six centre tanks, 16 wing tanks, and two slop tanks, all epoxy-coated. Stainless steel heating coils were fitted in all her tanks.

All the tanks had electro-hydraulic centrifugal submerged pumps, the centre tank pumps capable of moving 750 cu/m an hour, and the wing tank pumps 180 cu/m an hour. There was also an electro-hydraulic booster pump on deck for handling molasses.

Other features included the then newfangled Inmarsat phone and telex (the domes were becoming a new feature on ships' profiles), crude oil washing, inert gas system, segregated ballast tanks, double bottom, and bow thruster. Her main engine was an 11,200 bhp B&W from Mitsui, consuming 35 tn a day.

Founded in 1898, Mowinckels (it's perhaps a reflection of the importance of shipping to Norway that founder Johan Ludwig Mowinckel served three terms as Prime Minister) has operated tankers since 1926. It was involved in the Team Tankers pool (one of a number of product and chemical tanker pools at this time) with fellow Bergen owner Wallem, Steckmest & Co, as well as in dry bulk shipping as a major partner in the Gearbulk group.

Team Frosta – A/S J Ludwig Mowinckels Rederi, Norway; Sanoyasu Dockyard, Mizushima, 1981; 41,985 dwt, 184.51 m, 22 ta, 11,200 bhp Mitsui-B&W, 14.8 kn. (Tolerton)

No group of product tankers has had more unusual service than the five 29,500 dwt, 187 m ships of the American T-5 'Champion' class, of which *Gus W. Darnell* was the first completion. They were built for Military Sealift Command 20-year charters and completed in 1985-86 for the nominal ownership of Wilmington Trust Co. and managed by Ocean Ships of Houston. In 2003 the Military Sealift Command purchased four of the five. The aft sections of all five were built by Tampa Shipbuilding, Florida, and the cargo/forward sections by Avondale Shipyards, Louisiana, with *Gus W. Darnell* (launched as *Ocean Champion*, and the unwanted orphan when the other four were bought by MSC), *Paul Buck*, and *Samuel L. Cobb* being completed in 1985 and *Richard G. Matthiesen* and *Lawrence H. Gianella* in 1986. They were named after US merchant marine World War Two heroes. Whatever one's views on modern ship aesthetics, these were certainly rather ugly tankers, but state of the art with double hulls, inert gas, segregated ballast tanks, ice strengthening, and provision for stern discharge. They had 14 tanks each with its own pump, with a total handling capacity of 2741tn an hour. At least two, *Matthiesen* and *Gianella*, were set up for underway replenishment.

Each had a civilian crew of 24, and if most tanker crews complain about visiting the world's hottest ports, the seafarers on these ships could complain about the opposite. The ships carried fuel to the US McMurdo Sound research base in Antarctica (all five made voyages there) and also supplied the American Thule airbase in Greenland – the furthest north or south voyaging for product tankers – as well as US military bases around the world.

Richard G. Matthiesen – Wilmington Trust Co., as Trustee (Ocean Ships), USA; Tampa SB, Tampa (aft section) & Avondale Shipyards, Avondale (forward & cargo), 1986; 29,526 dwt, 187.43 m, 14 ta, 15,300 bhp IHI-Sulzer, 16 kn. (Tolerton)

Richard G. Matthiesen was a 1986 completion in the T-5 Champion class construction programme, and made the last voyage by one of this class to McMurdo, arriving there on January 26, 2011 with a year's supply of diesel, gas, and jet fuel. Fourteen cargo pumps could discharge 2741 tn an hour. Her underway replenishment gear is conspicuous.

One of the T-5 Champion class product tankers made the annual voyage to resupply McMurdo Station in Antarctica every southern summer for 26 years through to 2011. *Lawrence H. Gianella* is pictured approaching McMurdo (above). Berthing at the ice wharf at McMurdo in 2007 (below) is *Paul Buck*. Standing off her is the icebreaker *Polar Sea*, which has assisted her on her passage through the ice. Beyond these two ships is the American ice research ship *Nathaniel B. Palmer*, another regular visitor to Antarctica. An icebreaker assisted the tanker on the final stage of the passage each year.
(National Science Foundation photos)

The challenges of Antarctic navigation: Two views from the bridge of *Lawrence H. Gianella*, as the tanker butts through a Southern Ocean storm (below) and enters an ice channel (left) which has been opened up by an icebreaker. (photos: National Science Foundation)

The world's chemical tanker fleet grew enormously in the 1970s. Too fast in fact, and with a surplus of tonnage chemical tankers could readily compete for product cargoes. It was only in the 1960s that the first purpose-built parcel tankers were launched, but operators like Stolt-Nielsen, Westfal-Larsen, Odfjell, Ole Schroder, Essberger, and the Johnson Line started to specialise in parcel and chemical tankers and built up their fleets in the 1970s and early 80s, some of them also investing in storage and terminals around the world, too. Lean times in the chemical carrier trades sometimes saw the considerably more expensive and sophisticated chemical tankers slumming it and competing in the product trades, or carrying petroleum products as back cargoes or for repositioning voyages. Chemical tankers did not of course earn the same premium freights carrying product cargoes that they did for chemicals, and chemical tankers usually had 'one tank-one pump-one line' which was fine for multi-parcels of chemicals but less suitable for bulk discharge of petroleum products.

Torvanger – Malhar Shipping Corp (Westfal-Larsen & Co A/S), Liberia; Stocznia Szczecinska, Szczecin, 1976; 28,026 dwt, 170.52 m, 38 ta & 2 dk ta, 17,400 bhp Cegielski-Sulzer, 17 kn. (Tolerton)

One of the major chemical tankers orders of the 1970s was for twelve 28,000 ships for Norwegian owners Westfal-Larsen and Rederi Odfjell (six each). Built in Poland as the B76 class, they set a new benchmark for chemical tankers, with 16 stainless steel centre tanks, 22 wing tanks of zinc silicon-coated shipbuilding steel, and two stainless steel cylindrical deck tanks. There was a double bottom below each tank and the centre tanks had flush surfaces with the stiffeners on the exteriors. The ships were built 'one tank-one pump-one line' style, with each of the 38 tanks having a separate deepwell pump. Stainless steel was also used for all the pumps, ball valves, and lines, and the whole system was controlled remotely. With high-powered machinery for these 17kn ships, careful attention had to be given to preventing vibration affecting the cargo system. Originally Norwegian-flagged like her sisters, *Torvanger* (above) is illustrated after being reflagged to Liberia.

Essi Gina – K/S Skips A/S Essi Gina (Bj Ruud-Pedersen A/S), Norway; Nippon Kokan, Tsu, 1979; 16,529 dwt, 155.99 m, 28 ta, 11,200 bhp Mitsui-B&W, 16.75 kn. (Tolerton)

Something of a boutique operator in the chemical trades, Oslo owner Bjarne Ruud-Pedersen converted several bulk carriers to chemical tankers before commissioning the 16,529dwt *Essi Gina* from Nippon Kokan, supported by a long term charter to Associated Octel. She had eight centre tanks intended for antiknock compounds and 20 wing tanks for caustic. *Osco Sailor* of 1975 (below) was the last of four 34,000 dwt parcel tankers from Eriksbergs for Ole Schroder, another Oslo owner specialising in chemical tankers. She followed *Osco Stripe/Spirit/Sierra* of 1974, and had 36 tanks.

Osco Sailor – Product Trader Inc. (Osco Shipping A/S), Liberia; Eriksbergs, Gothenburg, 1975; 33,950 dwt, 171.81 m, 36 ta, 14,600 bhp Eriksbergs-B&W, 15.5 kn. (Tolerton)

State-of-the-art in product tankers – Concordia Maritime's new *Stena Impression* class ships started coming into service in 2015. (Concordia Maritime)

Modern Tankers

An enormous growth in size has been a feature of product tankers since the early 1990s. The old 30,000 dwt tanker has been replaced by 45,000 to 50,000 dwt tankers serving the same ports, and the largest product tankers are now up to nearly 120,000 dwt.

The world's product fleet breaks down into four broad categories, although, curiously, there are variations in the figures various maritime organisations quote for them. Intertanko's history 'A Century of Tankers' cites up to 35,000dwt as Handysize, 45,000 as Handymax, 55-80,000 as Large (sic) Range 1 (LR1), and 80-110,000 as LR2. 'Lloyd's List' categorises tankers 27-40,000dwt as Handymax, 40-50,000 as Medium Range (MR), 55-90,000 as Long (sic) Range 1/Panamax, and 90-120,000 as LR2/Aframax.

By mid-2009 about 210 LR2 tankers were in service. Hyundai Heavy Industries, the biggest builder of tankers, lists the construction of no fewer than 56 product tankers of around 100,000 dwt or more at its yards by the end of 2013, the first being a 99,999 dwt pair, *Torm Ann-Marie* and *Torm Helene*, delivered to Danish owner A/S D/S Torm companies in 1997 and the similar *Oriental Green* for Hyundai Merchant Marine in 1998, all three from HHI's Ulsan yard. The Torm pair are 243 m overall with 12 cargo tanks in six pairs in a double hull and able to handle four grades of cargo simultaneously with four steam turbine-driven centrifugal pumps that can each move 2000 cu/m an hour. A 16,681 bhp HHI-B&W engine offered 14 kn with fuel consumption of 42 tn a day.

The subsequent HHI completions of 100,000dwt or more included multiple deliveries to the Eletson Corporation, Tsakos Shipping & Trading, Teekay, India Steamship Co, Shipping Corporation of India, Novoship, and NYK. Notable at the top end for size are the 117,000 dwt Greek-flagged *Proteas*, *Promitheas*, and *Propontis* completed in 2006 for Tsakos, and similar *Polar Mariner* (now *Minerva Libra*) and *Polar Merchant* (now *Seamagic*) for Cypriot operator Interorient in 2007. These five ships are 249m overall and 44m wide, with of course double hulls, and heating coils, 12 cargo tanks and two slop tanks, and three pumps each capable of moving 3000 cu/m an hour. Machinery is a 22,800hp Hyundai MAN-B&W.

A notable early Korean order for six LR2 product giants came from Chandris (Hellas). Daewoo Heavy Industries delivered the 105,401dwt sisters *Astrea* and *Althea* from its Geoje yard to Chandris in 1999, and the Greek owner returned some years later to order four similar ships in the form of *Aktea* (2005) and *Athinea* (2006) from Daewoo and *Aegea* and *Amorea* (both 2009) from Samsung, Geoje.

Japanese yards have also built these product 'super tankers.' Namura Shipbuilding started construction of a number of LR2 ships of more than 100,000 dwt in the 1990s, including the 106,042dwt, 240.99m *Champion Peace* of 1999, with double hull and able to carry three types of products in her 12 cargo tanks served by three 2600 cu/m an hour pumps. Namura updated and improved its LR2 design for a new Aframax series starting with the 115,600dwt, 249.97m Hong Kong-flag sisters *FS Diligence* and *FS Endeavor* completed in 2012 at its Imari yard and also designed for three grades of cargo. They have radar-type tank level gauges for the cargo tanks, slop tanks, and residual slop tank, and the hull design incorporates Namura's energy-saving flow control fin device. The cargo tanks and pipes are, of course, pure epoxy coated for product carrying. Sumitomo Heavy Industries has built 105,400dwt double hull Aframax product carriers, including the *Unique Privilege* of 2003 which was sold to A.P. Moller in 2007 as *Maersk Privilege*, and *River Eternity* of 2006.

China has also contributed product tankers in this size range, with a notable early example being the 109,340 dwt, 244.48m, 15kn Greek flag *Seaqueen* from Dalian New Shipbuilding for Thenamaris in 1998. She has 12 cargo tanks in the usual six pairs within a double skin hull and three cargo pumps, each of which can move 3000 cu/m an hour. With double valve segregation throughout, three different cargoes can be carried. The engine is a 21,128hp Dalian-Sulzer.

Generally operating from refinery to refinery or refinery to major storage terminals, the Aframax giants are not going to be seen at most of the usual ports which host product tanker visits. Rather unusually, in August 2009 when there were 213 LR2 tankers in the global fleet, more than a quarter of them (60) were employed as storage ships off Rotterdam and elsewhere in Europe because of a lack of onshore storage at the time. Twenty-four of the 300 LR1s trading at the time were also employed this way.

Some typical voyaging for LR2 tankers is:

Torm Maren (109,672dwt/2008/Dalian Shipbuilding) – Zhoushan (8/2014), Singapore, Mina al Ahmadi, Chiba, Ulsan, Singapore, Jamnage Terminal (India), Mombasa, Ras Laffan, Agioi Theodosi, Antwerp, Mongstad (Norway), Nihama (Japan), Mizushima, Dalian, Jamnage Terminal, Cyprus (ship to ship transfer), Singapore, Jubail, Shell Haven (4/2015).

Propontis (117,055 dwt/2006/Hyundai) – Ust-Luga (Russia) (1/2014), Laundborg, Kaohsiung, Ust-Luga, Kalundborg, Ust-Luga, Skagen, Ust-Luga, Singapore, Mai-Liao (Taiwan), Kaohsiung, Daesan, Singapore, Shell Haven, Ust-Luga, Gwangyang, Daesan, Mai-Liao, Singapore, Fiumicino, Shell Haven, Ust-Luga, Mai-Liao, Ulsan (3/2015).

After decades in which Britain and Scandinavia, then Japan, dominated world tanker construction, South Korea has established itself this century as the world's largest builder of product tankers and of tankers generally, with the Hyundai Mipo Dockyard the leader in product tanker construction. In the first nine months of 2013, the yard received orders for 99 newbuildings, nearly 70 per cent of them being Medium Range product tankers representing more than 50 per cent of global orders. One of its notable completions is *STI Amber* for Scorpio Tankers in 2012, which it claimed as the world's first 'eco-design' MR tanker. Of 52,000dwt, the ship is designed to consume 20.5tn of fuel a day sailing laden at 13.5kn – nine tonnes (30.5 per cent) less than *Hellas Explorer* (ex-*STI Coral*) built to the same dimensions in 2008 at STX, Jinhae.

An overreaching consideration in the construction of modern product tankers has been the US Oil Pollution Act of 1990 (followed by the European Union's similar *Erika* anti-pollution legislation), which mandated that tankers trading in US waters from 2010 must have double bottom and double sides. As a result tankers with watertight double hulls — once just a bonus that made vessels more attractive for chartering -- have become universal. The American insistence on double hulls also contributed to the growth in the size of the typical handysize tanker from the 30,000-tonners of the past to today's longer and larger ships. As mentioned in the previous chapter, a few owners had commissioned double hull product tankers long before OPA, with a notable example and probably the first major order being the Eletson Corporation's order for a quartet of 46,000dwt vessels from Korea Shipbuilding (now Hanjin), Busan, which were delivered as

Samothraki, Psara, Halki (1989), and *Shinoussa* (1990). Eletson sold its last single-hulled vessel in 1996 to become probably the first tanker owner with an all double hull fleet. And between 1989 and 1996 Eletson ordered 15 Handymax and nine Panamax double-hulled product carriers.

The line between chemical tankers and product tankers has become blurred today, with many Handysize and MR tankers designed to carry IMO II or III-grade chemical cargoes as well as refined petroleum products, and being classified in the registers as "chemical/products" tankers. In 2013 Clarkson Research, the shipping intelligence specialist, revised its definition of product tanker to include chemical tankers of 30,000 to 59,999 dwt with at least one IMO II-graded tank, an average tank size of more than 3000 cu/m, and with tanks that are less than 75 per cent segregated. Tankers with stainless steel tanks remained classified as chemical tankers. "The reason for widening of the definition is the cargoes these tankers carry," announced Clarkson. "Principally, because of their tank size, these IMO II tankers are able to carry clean petroleum products, as well as vegetable oils. As the number of these vessels has increased, it is imperative to ensure that product tanker fleet definitions and statistics remain market relevant." Clarkson's statistics in December 2013 counted 286 IMO II product tankers with a combined deadweight of 13.2m in the overall product tanker fleet, with an average size of 46,327dwt for these ships, and 10.9m deadweight was in the 40,000 to 59,999dwt range. These IMO II tankers also had an average age of only 5.5 years against an overall average age of 9.3 for product tankers of more than 10,000 dwt. The fleet of this type had grown from 139 tankers at the beginning of 2008 to 254 at the beginning of 2013. Another 87 IMO II product tankers totaling 4.1m deadweight were on order at the end of 2013.

Another feature of today's product tanker fleet is the decline by the oil companies in designing their own classes of tankers, and the growing popularity, perhaps almost universal adoption, of shipyard standard designs. These vessels tend to be very similar, and the 'standard' Medium Range product tanker today, the workhorse of the product trades, is about 47,000dwt, with 'improved' versions stretching these designs up to 51,000 dwt. South Korea has set the pace in output, with China and Japan also contributing.

In the wake of pollution disasters like *Exxon Valdez, Erika,* and *Braer,* environmental considerations have of course become a key aspect of product tanker design, and no oil company would charter a vessel today that was not double-hulled. Improved standards of operation of chartered ships are also insisted upon by oil companies, and they carry out numerous safety audits and checklists to ensure high compliance levels with 'best practice' standards on vessels they charter. Obligatory fitting of inert gas plants has made today's tankers much safer, and many of the previous hazards to safety have been engineered out of modern tankers.

Ship-owning has always been a career for only the intrepid, and product cargo carriage, like every sphere of shipping, is cyclical, with the passage of the good and bad cycles for chartering interwoven with the consequences of building booms when owners rush to order new vessels when shipyard prices or market prospects look favourable. While the oil majors and large companies like A.P. Moller, Mitsui OSK, and NYK can ride through the ups and downs, it is a challenge to the inventiveness and experience of smaller operators to navigate successful through the leaner times. That came in 2009, for example, when some Medium Range product tanker owners were forced to accept charters at below break even levels (MR operating costs at the time were about $5000 a day).

In 2015 owners were looking ahead with cautious optimism, as new refineries in Saudi Arabia and at Ruwais, United Arab Emirates, mean more cargoes to be moved, the United States (now the world's largest product exporter, with the Middle East second) exporting record quantities in 2014, and exports from Russia expected to grow. And Australia faced a big increase in product imports after the closure of the Kurnell and Clyde refineries in Sydney and the Bulwer Island refinery in Brisbane, which cut that country's refining capacity by 42 per cent. Counterbalancing this, new launchings in 2015 and 2016 are forecast to create a fleet that will exceed the growth in product tanker demand. Operating product tankers, like most shipping businesses, is not for the faint-hearted.

Footnote: The Chinese 308,371 dwt very large crude carrier *Yuan Qiu Hu* carried possibly a world record products cargo on its maiden voyage in 2015. Owned by Dalian Cosco, the ship loaded a diesel cargo at the South Korean ports of Yosu and Gwangyang in early October 2015, and topped up at the Pengerang terminal in Malaysia. The diesel was for discharge at a West African port.

Astrea – Astrea Special Maritime Enterprise (Chandris (Hellas)), Greece; Daewoo HI, Geoje, 1999; 105,401 dwt, 248m, 12 ta & 2 slop ta, 19,101 hp Hyundai-MAN-B&W, 15.2 kn. (Tolerton)

Product tankers – but not as we know them. A feature of product tanker development in the last 20 or so years has been the evolution of vessels of 100,000dwt and more, a far remove from traditional product tankers. Early examples included the 105,000dwt Aframax sisters *Astrea* (above) and *Althea* of 1999 from Daewoo Heavy Industries for Chandris (Hellas) Inc. The company took delivery of four more of similar or slightly larger dimensions from Korean yards in the first decade of the new century. The 105,583dwt *Limerick Spirit* of 2007 (below) from Hyundai Heavy Industries, Ulsan, is one of a number of similar product carriers operated by Taurus Tankers, a subsidiary of Teekay Shipping operating LR2 tankers. She has three pumps each of 3000 cu/m an hour capacity.

Limerick Spirit – Limerick Spirit LLC (Teekay Shipping (Glasgow) Ltd), Bahamas; Hyundai HI, Ulsan, 2007; 105,583 dwt, 243.96 m, 12 ta & 2 slop ta, 18,420 hp Hyundai-MAN-B&W, 15 kn. (Taurus Tankers)

Torm Helene – Torm A/S, Denmark; Hyundai HI, Ulsan, 1997; 99,999 dwt, 243.74 m, 16,681 hp Hyundai-B&W, 14 kn. (Anton de Krieger)

Among Torm's LR2 product tankers is the 99,999 dwt *Torm Helene* (above), a 1997 completion from Hyundai, Ulsan, and by this time naturally built as a double-hull vessel. Four cargo pumps can each move 2000 cu/m per hour. Torm greatly expanded its fleet when it bought 26 product tankers owned by the Connecticut-based OMI Corporation (originally Ogden Marine Inc) in 2007, while Teekay Shipping took over OMI's nine Suezmax crude carriers and eight of its product tankers. The deal cost Teekay and Torm US $1.98 billion. Typical of OMI's modern fleet was the 46,922 dwt chemical-products carrier *Kansas* (below), completed by Hyundai Mipo in 2006, which was renamed *Torm Kansas* in 2008. Torm was given dispensation to reflag the Marshall Islands-registered OMI ships to Denmark.

Kansas – OMI Marine Services LLC, Marshall Islands; Hyundai Mipo, Ulsan, 2006; 46,922 dwt, 183.20 m, 13 ta & 2 slop ta, 11,840 bhp Hyundai-B&W, 14.5 kn. (Tolerton)

A.P. Moller/Maersk had the world's largest product tanker fleet after it acquired Brostrom Tankers for US $460m in January 2009 to add the Swedish company's 94 owned, chartered, or managed ships to its own fleet of 86 owned or chartered and 71 managed tankers – all product carriers apart from nine VLCCs. The acquisition gave Maersk a fleet of 242 product tankers of all sizes, with another 60 on order for delivery in the next four years. The world fleet at this time was around 3200 product tankers. Since then Maersk has disposed of its crude tankers (its VLCCs being sold in 2014), large gas carriers, and LNG ships, and concentrated its tanker interests on product carriers, affirming a commitment to them in spite of frightening multi-million dollar losses for its tanker division in 2012 and 2013. Additions to its product fleet in recent years include *Maersk Mikage* of 2009 (below), built to an Onomichi Dockyard 47,000 dwt standard design.

Maersk Mikage **– Sun God Navigation SA (Fuyo Kaiun Co), Panama; Onomichi Dockyard, Onomichi, 2009; 47,409dwt, 182.50 m, 12 ta & 2 slop ta, 11,665 hp Mitsui-MAN-B&W, 14 kn. (Onomichi Dockyard)**

Maersk Rhode Island – Maersk Line, USA; Guangzhou Shipyard International, Guangzhou, 2002; 34,801 dwt, 171.20 m, 12 ta, 12 tn cr, 8264 hp Dalian Marine-B&W, 14.5 kn. (Tolerton)

A prominent element of the Moller product fleet this century has been a class of 19 tankers of 34,900dwt completed by Guangzhou Shipyard and Dalian Shipbuilding in 1999-2004, starting with *Ras Maersk*. One of them, *Maersk Rhode Island* of 2002 (above), launched as *Maersk Ramsgate*, had the distinction of being Maersk's first American-flag tanker, being transferred to US registry in September 2002 with Norfolk as her home port and thus giving Maersk a timely foot in the door for American military or government cargoes at the expense of around an extra $6000 a day in manning costs. A more recent addition to the Moller fleet was the 48,020 dwt product carrier *Maersk Miyajima*, a 2011 completion from Iwagi Zosen (below).

Maersk Miyajima – Maxim Sunlight SA (Handytankers K/S), Panama; Iwagi Zosen, Kamijima, 2011; 48,020 dwt, 179.99 m, 12,889 hp Mitsui-MAN-B&W, 15 kn. (Tolerton)

Taganrog – Aurora Shipping & Trading Inc (Novoship (UK)), Liberia; Brodogradiliste Trogir, Trogir, 1996; 40,713 dwt, 181 m, 10 ta, 11,298 bhp Uljanik-B&W, 14.4 kn. (Tolerton)

Sovcomflot, operating crude carriers, shuttle tankers, gas tankers, and product carriers, dominates Russian tanker shipping, with the country's major product tanker operator, Novoship (Novorossiysk Shipping Co), merging with SCF in December 2007. The 40,713 dwt *Taganrog* (above) was one of at least a dozen similar Liberian-flagged ships built when Novoship renewed an aged fleet in the 1990s. Completed by Brodogradiliste Trogir in 1996, she was managed by the company's London-based subsidiary Novoship (UK), and displays the handsome Novoship funnel livery. More recent fleet upgrading saw the addition of 12 'Bridge' class ships from 2003 like the 47,185dwt *Transsib Bridge* of 2008 (below), built in St Petersburg, although earlier ships in the series came from Hyundai Mipo. She shows the Sovcomflot livery. The Bridges followed a class of eight 'Sea' ships built to similar dimensions in the late '90s.

Transsib Bridge – Hargate Marine Inc. (Unicom Management Services (Cyprus)), Liberia; Admiralteyskiy Sudostroitelnyy Zavod, St Petersburg, 2008; 47,185 dwt, 182.32 m, 10 ta & 2 slop ta, 11,298 hp Bryansk-MAN-B&W, 15 kn. (Anton de Krieger)

Ocean Venus – Da Guang Tankers (Pte) Ltd (Ocean Tankers), Singapore; SLS Shipbuilding, Tongyeong, 2006; 50,322 dwt, 189.02 m, 11 ta & 2 slop ta, 12,900 hp STX-MAN-B&W, 15 kn. (Tolerton)

Part of the Hin Leong Group, Ocean Tankers of Singapore grew steadily in the 1990s partly through the acquisition of some of Shell's old F class product tankers, and is now established as one of the major tanker companies after an extensive building programme this century which has seen it develop a large product tanker fleet as well as commissioning fourteen 318,000 dwt VLCCs. The 50,322 dwt *Ocean Venus* of 2006 from Korea's SLS Shipbuilding (above) is one of a series of 16 tankers completed in 2004 to 2009 that began with *Ocean Sunrise* of 2004, while the 41,340 dwt *Ocean Autumn*, also from SLS Shipbuilding, is one of four 'Four Seasons' sisters completed in 2009 at that shipyard. *Autumn* has a pump for each cargo tank but *Venus*, classified for products and crude cargoes, only three pumps.

Ocean Autumn – Xin Ying Shipping Pte Ltd (Ocean Tankers), Singapore; SLS Shipbuilding, Tongyeong, 2009; 41,340 dwt, 178.50 m, 12 ta & 2 slop ta, 11,665 hp Doosan-MAN-B&W, 15 kn. (Tolerton)

Stand-outs among the product tankers constructed in recent years have been the 10 innovative and very distinctive-looking P-Max ships constructed for Stena subsidiary Concordia Maritime of Gothenburg by Croatian shipbuilder Brodosplit. They are designed to carry clean or dirty products or crude, and at least five have been modified to IMO III class to also be able to carry vegetable oils and light chemicals.

The lead ship was *Stena Paris* which went into service late in 2005. She was followed by *Stena Provence* (2006), *Stena Primorsk* (2006), *Stena Performance* (2006), *Stena President* (2007), *Stena Perros* (2007), *Stena Progress* (2009), *Stena Polaris* (2010), *Stena Penguin* (2010), and *Stena Premium* (2011).

These 65,000 dwt tankers are 182 m long overall, but designed to load and carry considerably more cargo at ports and in waters with draught restrictions than comparable tankers of similar 13 m draught. They are much beamier with a moulded breadth of 40 m allowing them, say Concordia, to carry up to 30 per cent more on the same fuel consumption, and the scantlings make an interesting comparison with the typical product tankers of the 1970s carrying about 30,000 dwt on a length of 160 m overall.

The differences do not stop with their dimensions – the P-Maxs are all fitted with two MAN-B&W engines (each producing about 7860 kW) in separate enginerooms both with independent control and fuel systems, and with twin propellers and two independently controlled rudders. The bridge has 360 degrees visibility and a double control system, and navigation equipment includes automatic grounding avoidance. There are five pairs of epoxy-coated cargo tanks. The first ships in the series reportedly cost nearly US $35m each, with later vessels around US $44m.

In 2013, *Stena Polaris* (below) carried the first cargo to South Korea through the North East Passage in the Arctic Ocean, leaving the Russian port of Ust-Luga in the Gulf of Finland on September 17 carrying 44,000 tn of naptha and berthing at Yeosu on October 22. The Arctic passage meant a saving of about 10 days and 7000 km against sailing from northern Europe to Korea via Suez and the Indian Ocean. She has ten 800 cu/m an hour pumps for her 10 cargo tanks.

Stena Polaris – **CM P-Max VIII Ltd (Northern Marine Management), Bermuda; Brodosplit-Brodogradiliste, Split, 2010; 64,917 dwt, 182.99 m, 10 ta & 2 slop ta, 2 x Brodosplit-MAN-B&W 21,372 hp, 14.5 kn. (Tolerton)**

Stena Paris – CM P-Max Ltd (Northern Marine Management), Bermuda; Brodosplit-Brodogradiliste, Split, 2005; 65,125 dwt, 182.90 m, 10 ta & 2 slop ta, 2 x Brodosplit-MAN-B&W 21,372 hp, 14.5 kn. (Tolerton)

The first two ships of the series, *Stena Paris* (above) and *Stena Provence* (below), received French names in association with their initial five-year charters to French oil giant Total. They have 10 cargo tanks within, of course, a double hull and two slop tanks, and five pumps each capable of discharging 800 cu/m an hour. *Stena President* and subsequent vessels in the series had 10 pumps each of 800 cu/m an hour capacity. As can be seen from the photos, the bridges have 360 degrees visibility.

Stena Provence – CM P-Max II Ltd (Northern Marine Management), Bermuda; Brodosplit-Brodogradiliste, Split, 2006; 65,125 dwt, 182.90 m, 10 ta & 2 slop ta, 2 x Brodosplit-MAN-B&W 21,372 hp, 14.5 kn. (Tolerton)

Stena Bulk is following up the P-Maxs with a 10-ship 50,000 dwt IMO II chemical-product tanker series from Guangzhou Shipyard promoted as the IMOIIMAX class, with deliveries scheduled through into 2017 in a US $400m order. Like the P-Maxs, they are of dramatic appearance, and with an overall length of 183 m and 32 m beam, they are designed to carry clean or dirty petroleum products, chemicals, and vegetable oils in 18 phenolic epoxy-coated tanks each of 3000 cu/m capacity. Each tank is served by a deep well pump of 375 cu/m an hour capacity. The first vessel, the British-flagged *Stena Impression*, went into service early in 2015. She is owned by Stena Bulk and Singapore-listed Indonesian company Golden Agri-Resources, a major palm oil producer, and fitted with a nitrogen generator to use nitrogen inert gas in the cargo tanks instead of the traditional flue gas. They will operate in the Stena Weco pool which Stena and Danish company Dannebrog set up in 2011. Stena claims a 10 to 20 per cent fuel saving at service speed on ships of comparable size because of technical refinements that include main engine auto-tuning that sees each cylinder continuously automatically-controlled, an exhaust gas multi-inlet composite boiler that recovers energy from the exhaust gas of both the MAN main engine and the auxiliary engines, recovery of propeller energy loss via a hub vortex absorbing fin, and aerodynamic design of the accommodation and bridge block.

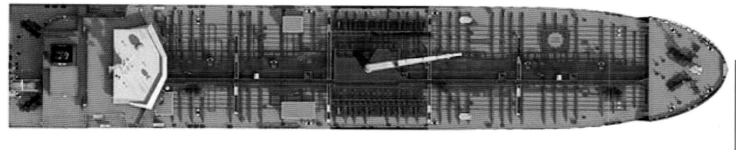

The fastest-growing product tanker fleet is owned by Monaco-based Scorpio Tankers, which grew into a major player in this segment of shipping by adding seven new ships in 2013 and, astonishingly, another 41 in 2014, with about 19 more new vessels scheduled for delivery in 2015 and 2016 – a remarkable show of confidence in the prospects for the product trades. In July 2016 it was operating 77 owned product tankers with an average age of 1.7 years plus 12 time-chartered ships. Scorpio also operates a bulk carrier fleet. Most, if not all, the product tanker orders have been from South Korean yards.

Listed on the New York Stock Exchange, Scorpio Tankers Inc is run by Emanuele Lauro, a grandson of one of the great Italian shipowners, Glauco Lolli-Ghetti, and his staff includes many executives from the former OMI group. A profit of US $39.3m for just the first calendar quarter of 2015 hints at why Scorpio is something of a darling of US investors. Many of the Scorpio tankers are named after London and New York suburbs with the prefix 'STI', the former recalling for people with both an interest in shipping and long memories the old tramp ship fleet of London owner Watts, Watts, & Co. One of the 2014 completions from Hyundai Mipo, *STI Pimlico*, was involved in a collision off Gallipoli with the cruise ship *Celestyal Crystal* in June 2015 while on passage from Tuapse (Russia) to Malta laden with naphtha.

In March 2015 Scorpio took delivery of the MRs *STI Pontiac* from Hyundai Mipo and *STI Manhattan* from another South Korean builder, SPP Shipbuilding, and the LR2 *STI Winnie* from Daewoo. What does a modern product tanker earn for its owners? On delivery *STI Pontiac* began a time charter for up to 120 days at about US $18,200 a day, *STI Manhattan* for up to 120 days at about US $19,600 a day, and *STI Winnie* a 55 day voyage at about $33,500 a day. A modern MR tanker costs about $8000 a day to run. In July 2015 Scorpio announced a more than $500 m order for up to 16 new product tankers which would take its fleet to more than 100. In February 2016 Scorpio sold five of its 2014-built Hyundai Mipo Eco MR tankers for US $166.5 m, the first time it had disposed of vessels from the Eco MR building programme.

STI Brixton – STI Brixton Shipping Co. (Claus-Peter Offen Tankschiffreederei), Marshall Islands; Hyundai Mipo, Ulsan, 2014; 38,734 dwt, 184 m, 14.45 kn. (Anton de Krieger)

Typical of Scorpio's modern tonnage is the oil and chemical tanker *STI Brixton* (above), a 2014 completion from Hyundai Mipo which commenced a 120 day charter at about $15,000 a day on delivery.

STI Acton – STI Acton Shipping Co (Scorpio Ship Management), Marshall Islands; Hyundai Mipo, Ulsan, 2014; 38,734 dwt, 184 m. (Anton de Krieger)

Two of the ships among Scorpio's enormous list of completions in 2014 which put the Monte Carlo company among the product tanker giants are *STI Acton* (above) and *STI Soho* (below). Both are chemical and oil products carriers, and like many ships in the Scorpio fleet, they have London place names – sometimes of rather unfashionable suburbs. Both also had at least a dozen sister ships in the Scorpio fleet in 2015, and like many bulk carriers and tankers today are registered in Majuro (Marshall Islands).

STI Soho – STI Soho Shipping Co (Zenith Gemi Isletmeciligi AS), Marshall Islands; SPP Shipbuilding, Tongyeong Shipyard, 2014; 50,140 dwt, 183 m. (Anton de Krieger)

Seven Express – **Seven Ocean Lines SA (Mitsui OSK Lines), Panama; Shin Kurushima Dockyard, Onishi, 2007; 45,998 dwt, 179.88 m, 14 ta & 2 slop ta, 12,599 hp Mitsubishi, 14.6 kn. (Tolerton)**

One shipping industry commentator scored Mitsui OSK as the biggest company in tanker shipping at the start of 2014, with a fleet of 15.8 m dwt including 40 VLCCs. This fleet also includes many product tankers, which with their 'Express' names, orange (generally) hulls and orange-red funnels are familiar in ports worldwide. The question of steam (well, motor) giving way to sail arose when the 45,998 dwt *Seven Express* (above) crossed tacks with more than 200 Optimist dinghies at the class's 2008 New Zealand championships. The ship is a 2007 completion from Shin Kurushima, and has three pumps each with 1000 cu/m an hour capacity to serve 14 tanks. The 45,798 dwt *Maple Express* (below), delivered by Minami-Nippon in 2002, is pictured passing one of Mitsui OSK's car carriers. She has four 950 cu/m an hour pumps for 12 tanks.

Maple Express – **East Harbour Shipping Ltd (Mitsui OSK Lines), Hong Kong; Minami-Nippon Zosen, Usuki, 2002; 45,798 dwt, 179.80 m, 12 ta & 2 slop ta, 11,640 hp Mitsui-B&W, 14.5 kn. (Tolerton)**

Emerald Express – Express Maritime Ltd (Mitsui OSK Lines), Marshall Islands; Onomichi Dockyard, Onomichi, 2011; 50,110 dwt, 182.50 m, 12 ta & 2 slop ta, 11,665 hp Mitsui-MAN-B&W, 14.8 kn. (Onomichi Dockyard)

The 50,110 dwt Majuro-registered *Emerald Express* of 2011 (above) is on the very long list of product tankers to come off the Onomichi Dockyard assembly line. A larger completion for MOL is the 74,998 dwt, Nassau-registered *Breezy Victoria* (below) in 2007 from Minami-Nippon. She has 12 tanks with three wing slop tanks, three cargo pumps each capable of handling 2000 cu/m an hour, and a 15tn hydraulic hose crane.

Breezy Victoria – Perennial Transport Inc (Mitsui OSK Lines), Bahamas; Minami-Nippon, Usuki, 2007; 74,998 dwt, 228 m, 12 ta & 3 slop ta, 15tn cr, 16,642 hp Mitsui-MAN-B&W, 14.9 kn. (Stephen Berry)

Challenge Premier – **NYK Bulkship (Asia) Pte Ltd (NYK Shipmanagement Pte), Singapore; Shin Kurushima, Onishi, 2005; 45,897 dwt, 179.88 m, 10 ta & 2 slop, 12,599 hp Kobe Hatsudoki-Mitsubishi, 15.1 kn. (Tolerton)**

Japan's other shipping giant, NYK, also has a large product tanker fleet, with its MR 'Challenge' types probably the most familiar in ports around the world. The Singapore-flagged 45,897dwt *Challenge Premier* (above), a 2005 completion from Shin Kurushima Dockyard, is one of a series of similar product tankers delivered to NYK from Shin Kurushima, Iwagi Zosen, and Onomichi, and she was sold to undisclosed buyers early in 2015 for US $16m. Cargo handling is via four pumps of 1000 cu/m an hour capacity. The 48,555 dwt *Challenge Prelude* (below), delivered from Iwagi Zosen in 2006, is another Singapore-registered ship of this general type but with six more tanks than *Premier*.

Challenge Prelude – **NYK Bulkship (Asia) Pte Ltd (NYK Line), Singapore; Iwagi Zosen, Kamijima, 2006; 48,555 dwt, 179.99 m, 16 ta & 2 slop ta, 12,889 hp Mitsui-MAN-B&W, 15.1 kn. (Tolerton)**

Hellespont Chieftain – mt Hellespont Chieftain GmbH & Co KG (Hellespont Ship Management GmbH & Co KG), Marshall Islands; Sekwang Shipbuilding, Mokpo, 2010; 16,850 dwt, 144 m, 14 ta & 2 slop ta, 8049 hp STX-MAN-B&W, 14.2 kn. (Anton de Krieger)

South Korea is now firmly established as the leader in product and chemical-product carrier construction. As well as the well-known giants, new yards have been developed this century, including SPP Shipbuilding's Tongyeong yard, which completed its first ship in 2006, and Sekwang Shipbuilding, Mokpo, with its first a year later. The 16,850 dwt *Hellespont Chieftain* of 2010 (above) from Sekwang is a fine example of the smaller chemical-products tanker today, and one of six sisters completed in 2009-10 in the Papachristidis-owned Hellespont fleet which has revived the old Onassis tradition of white-painted hulls. Majuro-registered, she has 14 cargo tanks each served by a pump of 300 cu/m an hour capacity. Among SPP's output has been six 50,000 dwt chemical-products tankers for Horizon Tankers of Piraeus of which the first was *Horizon Armonia* of 2008 (below). She also has a pump for each of her 12 cargo tanks, each of 600 cu/m an hour capacity.

Horizon Armonia – Boyero Shipping Ltd (Horizon Tankers), Liberia; SPP Shipbuilding, Tongyeong, 2008; 50,326 dwt, 183.09 m, 12 ta & 2 slop ta, 12,889 hp Doosan-MAN-B&W, 14.9 kn. (Tolerton)

BRO Albert – Brostrom Tankers SAS, France; Halla Engineering & Heavy Industries, Inchon, 1995; 45,999 dwt, 183.20 m, 8 ta & 2 slop ta, 10,150 hp Hyundai-B&W, 14 kn. (Tolerton)

Halla Engineering & Heavy Industries was the South Korean company most prominent in product tanker construction in the 1990s. The company was limited at its shipyard at Inchon, where there were tidal issues, to vessels of up to 50,000 dwt. Notable completions from Halla during the decade included six H class 47,000 dwt product tankers for Shell (see Shell chapter), and eight chemical-product carriers for the Van Ommeren group, all to an essentially similar standard design. At least 20 similar tankers for other owners were also built by Halla during the decade, making it one of the most successful designs of that time. The Van Ommeren ships, double-hulled chemical-products carriers and all completed with 'Port' names, had the prefix changed to 'BRO' in 2000. This followed Brostrom Shipping and Van Ommeren combining their product tanker interests in 1998, which entailed the Swedish company acquiring Dutch company VO's French tanker subsidiary. In 2009, as mentioned earlier in this chapter, Maersk took over Brostrom Tankers, and these ships later acquired a 'Maersk' prefix. Among them were *BRO Albert* of 1995 (above), named *Port Albert* until 2000 and having a sex change to *Maersk Claudia* in 2010, and *BRO Charlotte* of 1997 (below), which was similarly *Port Charlotte* and *Maersk Clarissa*.

BRO Charlotte – Societe en Commandite Simple 'Port Charlotte' (Brostrom Tankers SAS), France; Halla, Samho, 1997; 44,970 dwt, 180.80 m, 16 ta & 2 slop ta, 11,640 hp Hyundai-B&W, 14 kn. (Tolerton)

BRO Arthur – Brostrom Tankers SAS, France; Halla, Inchon, 1995; 46,801 dwt, 183.20 m, 8ta & 2 slop ta, 10,142 hp Hyundai-B&W, 14 kn. (Tolerton)

A feature which made these ships readily remembered by many observers was the port of registry on their sterns. Although the ownership was Dutch/Swedish, they were registered in Port-aux-Francais, the French Antarctic base in the Kerguelen Islands, and flew the French flag — as evidenced by *BRO Arthur* of 1995 (above). She became *Maersk Cameron* in 2010. She has eight cargo tanks served by eight pumps of 850 cu/m an hour capacity, although some of her sisters have 16 tanks. Among the similar Halla ships for other owners is the product tanker *Nedimar* of 1996 (below) for Stelmar Tankers, and named after the matriarch of the Haji-Ioannou clan, Nedi, mother of Stelmar owner Sir Stelios Haji-Ioannou. He sold Stelmar in 2005, and the ship was renamed *Overseas Nedimar* that year.

Nedimar – Nedimar Ltd (Stelmar Tankers), Cyprus; Halla, Inchon, 1996; 43,999 dwt, 183.20 m, 8 ta, 10,142 bhp Hyundai-B&W, 14.5 kn. (Tolerton)

Hellas Fos – Monroe Maritime SA (Consolidated Marine Management), Greece; Hyundai, Ulsan, 1999; 46,168 dwt, 183.20 m, 12 ta & 2 slop ta, 10,440 hp Hyundai-MAN-B&W, 14.2 kn. (Tolerton)

Hyundai Heavy Industries is now well established as the world's biggest tanker builder (as well as the world's biggest shipbuilding company), and here are some examples of its product tanker tonnage. *Hellas Fos* of 1999 (above) from HHI's Ulsan yard was an example of the 46,000 dwt output at the time – one of seven similar ships for its Greek owners, and not to be confused with the 1979 French-built giant *Hellas Fos*, at 555,000 dwt, one of the largest tankers ever built. The 1999 vessel was sold in 2005 to become *Dauntless,* and again in 2010 to become *Admiral 8*. HHI subsequently built yet another *Hellas Fos*, an LPG tanker, at Ulsan in 2008. *Iran Faraz* of 2004 (below) was one of a 35,000 dwt chemical-products pair from the Ulsan yard for the National Iranian Tanker Corporation. Hyundai Mipo is HHI's product tanker niche yard.

Iran Faraz – NITC, Iran; Hyundai Mipo, Ulsan, 2004; 35,155 dwt, 175.93 m, 15 ta, 11,640 hp Hyundai-B&W, 15 kn. (Tolerton)

Ardmore Seafarer – **Fastnet Shipco LLC (Ardmore Shipping), Marshall Islands; Minami-Nippon, Usuki, 2004; 45,744 dwt, 179.80m, 12 ta & 2 slop, 11,665 hp Mitsui-B&W, 14.5 kn. (Tolerton)**

Minami-Nippon Zosen has also been building product tankers, including the 45,744 dwt *Ardmore Seafarer* (above), a product carrier built in 2004 as *Zao Express* but since 2010 in the fleet of a product shipping high flyer, the Cork-based Ardmore Shipping Corporation. The company has flourished under president and CEO Anthony Gurnee and chairman Reginald Jones since its establishment in 2010, and in mid-2015 had a modern fleet of 19 MR product and chemical-products tankers, with another five on order. Of vaguer provenance is the intriguingly named *Patagonian Mystic* of 2005 (below), a flush-decked Panamanian-flagged chemicals and products carrier, which is one of a number of similar MR tankers from Naikai Zosen. She has the typical modern tank configuration of 12 cargo tanks and two slop tanks.

Patagonian Mystic – **New Seagull Shipping SA (Bernhard Schulte Shipmanagement (Singapore)), Panama; Naikai Zosen (Setoda Shipyard), Onomichi, 2005; 49,414 dwt, 186 m, 12 ta & 2 slop, 12,889 hp Hitachi-B&W, 14.6 kn. (Tolerton)**

Hinea – Shell Bermuda (Overseas) Ltd, UK; Vickers-Armstrongs, Barrow, 1956; 19,246 dwt, 169.42 m, 33 ta & 1 ha, 3x5 tn & 4x1 tn der, 2 Vickers Armstrongs stm turbs 8250 shp, 15.25 kn. (K Barr/R A Priest collection)

Nearly 90 tankers were completed for Shell in its H, K, and A class building programme from 1953 into the early 1960s, including *Hinea* of 1956 (above). A later generation of Shell product tankers included *Entalina* of 1978 (below), one of the E class built at the Saint John shipyard in New Brunswick, Canada.

Entalina – Shell Bermuda (Overseas) Ltd, UK; Saint John SB & DD Co, Saint John NB, 1978; 31,486 dwt, 169.45 m, 21 ta, 12,000 bhp Sulzer, 14.5 kn. (Tolerton)

Shell's Product Tankers

In the early 1950s the Shell group embarked on a large newbuilding programme of 18,000 dwt, general purpose tankers, and the resulting H, K and A class ships, numbering nearly 90, were familiar visitors in most ports of the world during the next two decades.

Ordered in 1951, a total of 65 were delivered between 1953 and 1959. General particulars of the class were: 169.38 m length overall, 161.54 m length bp, 21.15 m beam, 9.35 m summer draught. Gross tonnage was 12,190, net tonnage 6970, deadweight carrying capacity about 19,200 tonnes. Powered by geared steam turbines driving a single screw, service shp was 7500 giving a propeller speed of 100 rpm, producing a loaded service speed of 14.5 kn and 15.25 kn in ballast. Fuel oil consumption was 50 tn a day. Steam was supplied by two water-tube boilers at 500 psi pressure.

All 33 cargo tanks (11 sets of port, centre, and starboard) were fitted with steam heating coils. Cargo was discharged by four 500 cu/m an hour vertical centrifugal cargo pumps, driven by steam turbines. The cargo pipeline system was a double ring main, to obtain with one pumproom aft the same flexibility as was normal with two pumprooms, and a 10 inch stern discharge pipeline was fitted. Water ballast was able to be carried in the forepeak, forward cofferdam, and aft peak, a total capacity of about 500 tn, and inadequate for seagoing conditions, so cargo tanks needed to be ballasted with seawater. Fuel oil bunkers were carried in the forward deep tank and in wing bunkers, settling tanks and double bottoms aft, a total capacity of about 1650 tn.

Earlier Shell had its 'Three 12s' which were mainly built during World War Two, including the N class, which continued for a few years after the war. Like BP's similar ships, they had diesel main engines and steam-reciprocating cargo pumps.

When Shell built the H and K class from 1953, the ships were fitted, mainly, with steam-turbine main engines, at a period when oil was cheap. But they had an overlooked advantage over the BP tankers built at the same time, and that was their cargo pumps — often regarded as the commercial lifeblood of a tanker operation. The H, K, and later streamlined A class all had steam turbine-powered centrifugal cargo pumps, usually four, all fitted in an aft pump room. This enabled superheated steam to be used within the engine room to power the cargo pumps sited in the pump room, in a flat below the engine room. Higher cargo discharge rates were able to be achieved, and more importantly, a steady discharge pressure was able to be maintained, rather than the pulsating pressures created by reciprocating pumps, which could put more stress on the shore pipelines.

In the days before portable hand-held radios were in use, on the H class, the steam-turbine driven centrifugal cargo pumps had to be started locally in the engine room by the duty engineer before being given over to control from the pump room. "Requests" to start them were communicated by banging on the pump room bulkhead with a large (brass and spark-proof) hammer, so that the duty engineer could start them. This was best heard after completion of discharge and after the cargo surveyor had certified that all tanks were empty. The cargo pumps were then used to pump seawater-ballast in from the sea into the cargo tanks. Thus, it was "bang", "bang-bang", "bang-bang-bang" and "bang-bang-bang-bang" so that the pumps could roar into life again. Ballasting took about three hours, and standard ballast was about 25 per cent of the tanker's deadweight capacity. In the days before inert gas systems, during the ballasting operations, ex-petrol tanks being ballasted would show a shimmering gas plume exiting the vents at the top of the tank! It is much different today, with segregated ballast tanks and inert gas systems in the cargo tanks.

One subtle way of knowing which types of pumps a tanker had was where the pump room(s) were sited. It is not possible to pipe superheated steam along a deck steam line to an amidships pump room to operate centrifugal pumps. Thus, if a tanker had a pump room just aft or just forward of the amidships accommodation, then she had steam reciprocating pumps. If not, she likely had centrifugal pumps aft. Turbine centrifugal pumps also needed less maintenance work than reciprocating pumps.

As tankers became larger, more and more had centrifugal pumps aft. Bitumen tankers retained reciprocating pumps because of the viscosity of that cargo, as did some early parcels tankers. Centrifugal pumps needed more care and attention during discharge than reciprocating pumps, and needed to be slowed down when emptying the tank, whereas reciprocating pumps could bang away until the tank was empty and the pump was sucking air before stopping or changing over to the next tank.

When the cost of bunker fuel increased and motor tankers became more economical to operate again, they needed to be fitted with some type of steam boiler to operate their steam turbine-powered cargo pumps. Later, as technology further progressed, tankers changed to hydraulic-powered cargo pumps powered by power-packs, thereby negating the need for steam or boilers. The same reasons caused a change from steam-powered mooring winches fore and aft, which all became hydraulically-powered.

The H, K, and As also had a dry cargo hold, sited over the forward deep tank. It had 22,140 cu/ft bale capacity and was worked by a 5 tn derrick on the foremast, through a hatch eight feet square, which was large enough for slings of six drums. The small forward pump room, part of the cofferdam, contained two small steam pumps, one for transferring bunkers from the deep tank, and the other for handling ballast from the forepeak and cofferdam.

The forecastle contained the paint store, whilst the centrecastle space, under the midships accommodation, contained the mate's, bonded, stewards, canvas and deck stores. At the aft end was a small lamp store, where the emergency brass oil lamps were stored. Aft of midships, port and starboard, were the Samson posts with 5tn derricks for handling cargo hoses or stores. The windlass, fore deck, and main deck winches were steam driven, and two steam driven warping capstans were fitted on the poop. Standard navigation equipment was a radar, gyro and magnetic compass, echo sounder, and Decca Navigator.

They were designed as general-purpose ("GP") tankers and carried white oils, crudes, black oils, lubricating oils, and in some cases, wax and bitumen. Cargo tanks were unpainted, so they tended to stay in white or black oil trades for long periods, as extensive tank cleaning was required to change from black to white.

Four of the ships, the British *Helix* and *Helcion* and Dutch *Koratia* and *Korenia*, differed in having turbo-electric machinery.

The British-flag tankers in order of completion were:
Harpa (1953, Harland & Wolff, Belfast), *Helix* (1953, Swan Hunter & Wigham Richardson, Wallsend), *Hemidonax* (1953, Cammell Laird, Birkenhead), *Helcion* (1954, Swan Hunter, Newcastle), *Haustrum* (1954, Hawthorn Leslie, Newcastle), *Hemifusus* (1954, Cammell Laird), *Hadra* (1954, Smith's Dock, Middlesbrough), *Haustellum* (1954, Hawthorn Leslie), *Hyria* (1954, Lithgows, Port Glasgow), *Hadriania* (1954, Smith's Dock), *Hemiglypta* (1955, Cammell Laird), *Hyala* (1955, Lithgows), *Hemiplecta* (1955, Cammell Laird), *Haminea* (1955, Smith's Dock), *Hindsia* (1955, Vickers Armstrong, Barrow), *Harpula* (1955, H&W, Belfast), *Heldia* (1955, Swan Hunter, Wallsend), *Hinea* (1956, Vickers Armstrong, Barrow), *Hygromia* (1956, Lithgows), *Hinnites* (Vickers Armstrong, Newcastle), *Horomya* (1956, Hawthorn Leslie), *Harvella* (1956, Harland & Wolff, Belfast), *Hatasia* (1956 J L Thompson, Sunderland), *Helisoma* (1956, Swan Hunter, Wallsend), *Hydatina* (1956, Lithgows), *Hima* (1957, Odense Staalskibs, Odense), *Haminella* (1957, Smith's Dock), *Hemisinus* (1957, Cammell Laird), *Hanetia* (1957, Smith's Dock), *Halia* (1958, Hawthorn Leslie).

The Shell group acquired its long-established rival Eagle Oil and the Eagle Tanker Co fleet in 1959, and its H class tankers swapped their Mexican saints names for Shell names in 1964-65.

These vessels were: *Hemidonax* (ex-*San Florentino*, from Cammell Laird, 1953), *Hemicardium* (ex-*San Fernando*, Cammell Laird, 1953), *Hastula* (ex-*San Fabian*, Smith's Dock, 1956), *Hemimactra* (ex-*San Fortunato*, Cammell Laird, 1956), *Holospira* (ex-*San Felipe*, Smith's Dock, 1956), and *Hemitro-chus* (ex-*San Emiliano*, Cammell Laird, 1959). A tanker which did not survive to join the Shell fleet was *San Flaviano*, built in 1956 at Cammell Laird and sunk by air attack at Balik Papan on April 28, 1958, during the Indonesian civil war.

Shell took over another 18,000 dwt Eagle tanker, *San Edmundo* of 1958, from Furness Shipbuilding, Haverton Hill, and renamed *Humilaria* in 1964. However, this steamship had been ordered for other owners and was not of the standard H class design, being purchased by Eagle while building.

Like the Blue Funnel Line's, Shell's ship names provoked the humour of seafarers and dockers, with a prime example being the H class *Hinnites*, inevitably known as the 'honeymoon ship.' However, they also generated an affection and there were instances of staff bestowing Shell names on their new-borns, such as *Darina*, *Velletia*, *Melania*, and *Venassa* (not the usual Vanessa). One can presume that some may have been the ships on which they were conceived.

The Dutch flag completions in order were:

Katelysia (1954, Rotterdam Drydock, Rotterdam), *Koratia* (1954, Wilton-Fijenoord, Schiedam), *Korovina* (1954, Wilton-Fijenoord), *Krebsia* (1954, P Smit Jr, Rotterdam), *Kalydon* (1955, Rotterdam Drydock), *Kenia* (1955, Netherlands Dock, Amsterdam), *Kabylia* (1955, Rotterdam Drydock), *Kore-nia* (1955, Wilton-Fijenoord), *Kryptos* (1955, P Smit), *Kylix* (1955, Netherlands Dock), *Kermia* (1955, Netherlands Dock), *Kopionella* (1955, Wilton-Fijenoord), *Kara* (1955, Netherlands Dock), *Khasiella* (1956, Netherlands Dock), *Kosicia* (1957, S A Cockerill-Ougree, Hoboken), *Kelletia* (1957, Rotterdam Drydock).

Two more were completed to sail under the French flag: *Iphigenia* (1955, Chant. Navals de la Ciotat, La Ciotat), and *Iridina* (1955, Chant. Navals).

The H and K-type tankers completed for non-Shell companies but mostly demise-chartered to Shell were:

Cerinthus (1954, from Harland & Wolff, for Hadley Shipping), *Forthfield* (1955, from Hawthorn Leslie, for Huntings), *Eastgate* (1957, from J L Thompson, for Turnbull Scott), *Westertoren* (1954, from Rotterdam Drydock, for Nederlandse Tank & Paketv.), *Schelpwijk* (1955, from De Schelde, for NV Stoomvaart Maats. 'Oisterwijk'), *Kaap Hoorn* (1958, from Netherlands Dock, for NV Stoomv. Maats. 'Nederland'), *Lucellum* (1958, from Cammell Laird, for Cunard), *Dorestad* (1955, from Netherlands Dock, for Amsterdamsche Olietransport), *Ameland* (1956, from P. Smit, for Rotterdam SS), *Purmerend* (1957, from Netherlands Dock, for Amsterdamse Maritiem Transport), *Munttoren* (1957, from Van der Giessen-De Noord, for Nederlandsche Tank & Paketv.), *Alkmaar* (1958, from Netherlands Dock, for Amsterdamse Maritiem Transport).

Some representative voyages of the H class:

Heldia (April 1967-January 1968): Singapore – Penang – Pladju – Singapore – Woodlands – Singapore – Bangkok – Singapore – Auckland – Lyttelton - Balik Papan – Singapore – Pladju – Singapore – Bangkok – Singapore – Woodlands – Bangkok – Singapore – Woodlands - Port Dickson – Penang - Port Dickson – Singapore – Lae – Rabaul – Madang – Pladju – Singapore – Darwin – Dampier – Fremantle – Singapore – Woodlands – Bangkok – Pladju – Singapore - Port Dickson – Penang – Dubai - Bandar Mashur - Lourenco Marques – Aden – Singapore – Surabaya – Pladju – Singapore – Woodlands - Mena Al Ahmadi - Bandar Mashur – Mauritius - Dar es Salaam - Bandar Mashur. (63,612 miles, 291,702 tonnes)

Hemimactra (June-December 1974): Shellhaven – Arzew – Rotterdam – Huelva – Rotterdam – Shellhaven – Rotterdam – Gibraltar – Tunis – Malta – Piraeus – Arzew – Rotterdam – Hamble - Le Havre – Stanlow – Eastham – Dingle – Ardrossan – Eastham – Rotterdam – Nordenham – Hamburg – Brunsbuttel – Holtenau – Fredericia – Copenhagen - Milford Haven – Avonmouth – Stanlow – Eastham – Dublin – Avonmouth – Curacao – Kingston - Port Rhodes – Curacao - Panama Canal – Balboa - Panama Canal – Curacao – Cardon - Santo Thomas De Castilla – Curacao – Cristobal - Panama Canal

- Puerto Armuelles – Golfito - Panama Canal – Almirante – Cardon - Santo Thomas De Castilla – Curacao - Caracas Bay – Cristobal - Balboa. (31,536 miles, 336,901 tonnes)

Hima (September 1964-March 1965): Port-De-Bouc – Malta – Tobruk – Piraeus – Milazzo - La Spezia – Lisbon – Stanlow – Curacao – Cardon – Luanda - Ango Ango – Curacao – Casablanca – Gibraltar – Algiers – Bone – Port-De-Bouc – Naples – Malta – Piraeus – Larnaca – Port Said – Abadan - Lourenco Marques – Beira – Abadan - Lourenco Marques - Aden. (45,702 miles, 109,962 tonnes)

Hinnites (May-November 1965): Thameshaven - Isle of Grain – Stanlow – Dublin – Ardrossan – Whitegate – Dublin – Heysham – Hamble – Europoort – Pernis – Gothenburg – Pauillac – Donges – Rotterdam – Thameshaven – Shellhaven - Old Kilpatrick – Dingle – Stanlow – Dingle – Stanlow – Avonmouth – Stanlow – Killingholme – Cardon - New York – Curacao – Cardon – Recife - Rio de Janeiro – Santos - Rio Grande – Cardon – Curacao – Rotterdam - Thameshaven. (29,467 miles, 252,800 tonnes)

The H and Ks were followed by the streamlined A class. These were: *Abida* (1958, from P Smit), *Amastra* (1958, from Smith's Dock), *Acila* (1958, from P Smit), *Acavus* (1958, from Bremer Vulkan, Vegesack), *Achatina* (1958, from Bremer Vulkan), *Axina* (1958, from Lithgows), *Arca* (1959, from Rotterdam Drydock), *Anadara* (1959, from Hawthorn Leslie), *Asprella* (1959, from Kieler Howald-swerke, Kiel), *Acmaea* (1959, from P Smit), *Aulica* (1960, from Kieler Howaldswerke), *Atys* (1960, from Netherlands Dock), *Amoria* (1960, from Smith's Dock), *Acteon* (1961, from P Smit). Flag followed the nation of build for all these vessels, apart from the four German completions which were for Shell's British flag fleet. *Abida, Acila, Arca, Acmaea, Amoria,* and *Acteon* were motorships and the others steamships.

Only one streamlined type was built for Eagle Oil, this was the steamship *Alinda* (ex-*San Ernesto*) completed by Smith's Dock in 1959. Three of the streamlined type were completed for non-Shell companies but mostly demise-chartered to Shell: *Vlieland* (steam, 1959, from Wilton-Fijenoord, for Rotterdam SS), *Stonegate* (motor, 1961, from Smith's Dock, for Turnbull Scott), *Clymene* (steam, 1961, from Hawthorn Leslie, for Hadley Shipping).

Two others similar to the streamlined type were built by Deutsche Werft, Hamburg, in 1959 as bitumen tankers, *Pallium* and *Partula*. Externally their appearance was similar, but their hulls were two feet wider, with the centre tanks wider and the wings tanks narrower than the standard design, bitumen being carried in the centre tanks only, and ballast in the wings. Thus, the total on the same hull design was 85.

Not to be confused with the class were *Helicina* (1946) and *Hyalina* (1948) which although of similar nomenclature, were totally different ships. Similarly, *Aluco* and *Arianta* of 1959 should not be confused with the rest of the A class, being of all-aft design and having a different hull. They were also built as white oil product tankers, and were not "general purpose."

The move by other British companies to take sister vessels to the H class had been encouraged by Cyril Warwick of Houlder Bros on behalf of Shell, and with the inducement of long-term charters it is unlikely they regretted it.

Well-known tramp ship operator Turnbull Scott & Co., for example, was persuaded to take up a building contract Shell had placed with Joseph L. Thompson & Sons, the purchase deal including a 20-year bareboat time charter back to Shell. The steam turbine tanker *Eastgate* was launched in 1957, carrying clean oils for the first two years, then into the 'dirty' trades carrying mainly fuel oil or diesel oil, before having her tanks cleaned and reverting to clean trading in 1966.

In the meantime Turnbull Scott had also taken the streamlined A class-type *Stonegate*, a motor-ship, from Smith's Dock in 1960, again on a 20-year bareboat time charter to Shell and going into service for the clean trades.

The H and Ks were mostly disposed of by Shell to other owners or the breakers' yards in 1972-75 as a downturn in the tanker market kicked in.

Shell supplemented its product tanker fleet by the conversion in 1970 of *Varicella* (21,843 gross, 34,395 dwt, built 1959) to carry white oils in 1970. She later carried grain from the US to Turkey in

August 1974. She was later sold to Singapore owners, renamed *Cherry Baron* and used as a storage tanker in Singapore Roads. She arrived at Kaohsiung in tow in April 1983 for scrapping.

By the early 1970s it was deemed necessary to consider replacements for the older ships, which were shortly to reach the end of their lives. In the years since their building, increased oil consumption had led to an increase in the size of product tankers, and a standard size of approximately 32,000 dwt was decided on.

The first group of nine tankers was built by Haugesund Mekaniske Verksted, Haugesund, Norway, as yard numbers 48-56 in an order worth more than £47 million placed by Shell International Marine Ltd. First to be completed was *Fjordshell* in February 1974, for A/S Shell Baatane, Norway, for coastal trading in Scandinavian waters, and differed in construction and equipment from the following eight ships because of her design for coastal trading.

The accommodation had one deck less due to a smaller crew allowed under Norwegian law, and a bow thruster assisted berthing operations. Tonnages were 18,625 gross and 32,465 dwt, with a Sulzer 10,500 bhp main engine. Her initial intended name was *Faunus*, but this was changed to suit the coastal trading area.

The remainder of the ships were true sisters, and entered service as *Fulgur* (October 1974), *Felania* (February 1975), *Fusus* (May 1975), *Felipes* (November 1975), *Ficus* (February 1976), *Flammulina* (April 1976), *Fossarina* (October 1976), and *Fossarus* (December 1976). Registered owners were either Citizens Trust Co. or United States Trust Co., on demise charter to Shell International Petroleum Co.

When built, *Fulgur*, *Felania*, *Fossarina*, and *Fossarus* were manned and managed by Shell Tankers BV (Netherlands),whilst *Fusus*, *Felipes*, *Ficus*, and *Flammulina* were managed and manned by Shell Tankers (UK) Ltd.

All eight were registered under the Liberian flag. All nine F class had dimensions of 170.69 m length overall, 25.94m beam and except for *Fjordshell*, were 19,275 gross and 32,230 dwt on a summer draught of 11.37 m. Main engines were two 6 cyl.MAN diesels driving a four-blade controllable pitch propeller via flexible couplings and reduction gearbox. Two A.E.G. generators, coupled via power take-off drive to the gearbox, supplied power for four 900 cu/m an hour electric cargo pumps, and power to a high pressure hydraulic system for drive of all mooring winches, anchor windlasses, and the deck crane. The ships were designed for white oils only, and lack of heating coils allowed a simplified machinery layout, with no steam-raising plant.

The second group of tankers was built by St. Johns Shipbuilding & Drydock Co. Ltd, St. John, New Brunswick, Canada, as yard numbers 1119-1123. First to be completed was *Erinna* (October 1977), followed by *Etrema* (March 1978), *Entalina* (July 1978), *Erodona* (November 1979), *Ensis* (January 1979), and *Elona* (May 1979).

The first four were managed by Shell Bermuda Overseas Ltd, managed and manned by Shell Tankers (UK) Ltd, under British flag, while the last two were owned by Lepton Shipping Corp, managed and manned by Deutsche Shell Tanker GmbH, under Liberian flag. Main engines were a single Sulzer 6RND76, providing 12,000 bhp and driving a four-blade controllable pitch propeller, giving an average speed of 14.75kn. Two vertical Sunrod boilers provided steam for cargo heating, mooring and anchoring windlasses, and four x 900 cu/m an hour cargo pumps. All had dimensions of 169.30m length overall, 26.07 m beam, and were 19,656 gross and 30,990 dwt on a summer draught of 10.92 m.

The third group of four tankers were built by Mitsui Engineering & Shipbuilding Co. Ltd, Chiba, Japan, as yard numbers 1123-1126. First to be completed was *Eburna* (January 1979), followed by *Ervilia* (June 1979), *Euplecta* (January 1980), and *Ebalina* (May 1980). All were owned, managed and manned by Shell Tankers (UK) Ltd under British flag.

Main engine was a single 6 cyl. Mitsui B.&W. DE 6L67GFC, providing 11,200 bhp and driving a four-bladed controllable pitch propeller giving an average speed of 14.75 kn. Two vertical Sunrod boilers provided steam for the same services as the other E class. The four Mitsui ships were the result of a renegotiated contract for yard number 1049, a 310,991dwt ULCC, which would have been the fourth such ship from Mitsui for Shell after *Lanistes*, *Laconica*, and *Litiopa*.

Although differing in details, all the F and E class had common standards. All engine spaces were highly automated, worked from a central control room, and designed for unmanned operation, with direct bridge control of the engines. All had seven sets of port, centre, and starboard cargo tanks, giving 21 in total, except the Mitsui Es, which had No.2 centre and 4 centre subdivided to give a total of 23 tanks. The aftermost wing tanks were used as slop tanks for tank-cleaning purposes.

All cargo tanks and pipelines were fully painted with epoxy or zinc, and all cargo pumps were self-priming and able to fully drain without separate stripping pumps and lines. All cargo valves were hydraulically controlled from mimic displays in the cargo control room, from where pump speeds and discharge pressures were controlled, and where tank levels, cargo temperature, and hull draught were displayed.

All crew members had separate cabins with private facilities, and all cabins were above poop deck level, making the accommodation block high in appearance. Although total accommodation for between 35 and 45 was provided (including shoreworkers' cabins and spare berths), the normal complement (excluding cadets and trainees) was about mid-20s.

When they entered service they were engaged in worldwide trading based mainly from the Singapore, Curacao, and Rotterdam refineries. In oil trade jargon, they were known as MRXs, the MR indicating Medium Range size, and the X to differentiate from earlier tankers of a similar deadweight, but with a length of up to 210 m, and unable to use some of the ports used by MRXs. With a length the same as the 18,000 dwt tankers they replaced they were able to use the same berths, carrying more cargo for the same length when depths permitted, or deadfreighting when depth restrictions applied. It was an indication of the rate of change of the tanker world that only 20 years earlier, this size of tanker was being introduced as the latest standard-size supertanker for carrying single grades of crude oil.

Some typical voyaging of the E class:

Ebalina (February-March 1982) – Singapore – Pulau Sambu – Surabaya – Singapore – Hong Kong – Singapore – Hong Kong – Singapore – Hong Kong – Singapore – Bangkok – Singapore. (12,064 miles carrying 155,595 tonnes)

Entalina (September 1979-January 1980) -- Singapore – Port Hedland – Dampier – Singapore – Hong Kong – Singapore – Yokohama – Singapore – Darwin – Wyndham – Singapore – Anewa Bay – Honiara – Lae – Singapore – Jurong anchorage. (28,125 miles carrying 190,815 tonnes)

Erinna (July-October 1978) – Dakar – Lagos – Dakar – Lagos – Curacao – Sal – Dakar - Banjul – Monrovia – Cotonou – Doula – Port Gentil – Freetown – Las Palmas – Hamburg – Rotterdam. (20,766 miles, carrying 73,273 tonnes)

Ervilia (July-November 1982) – Wellington – Auckland – Westernport – Teluk Semangka – Singapore – Chittagong – Singapore – Lyttelton – Auckland – Singapore – Teluk Semangka – Jakarta – Singapore – Sriracha – Bangkok – Singapore – Wellington – Bluff – Dunedin. (29,742 miles, carrying 184,048 tonnes).

Shell's next class of product tankers was standard 47,000 dwt tankers built by Halla Engineering & Heavy Industries, Inchon, between 1993 and 1994 as *Halia* (August 1993), *Hastula* (October 1993), *Hatasia* (December 1993), *Haustrum* (February 1994), *Hadra* (March 1994), and *Haminea* (June 1994). They were all 28,277 gross tonnage, 46,850 dwt, with a length overall of 183.2 m, beam of 32.23m, and summer draught of 12.26 m. At various times they were Liberian, Dutch, or Isle of Man registered.

The next three were the *Fusus*, *Ficus*, and *Fulgur*, built in 2001 by Brodosplit Shipyard Ltd, Split, all 27,542 gross tonnage and 44,787 dwt, with length overall of 183.4 m, 32.3 m beam, and 12 m summer draught. All three were Isle of Man registered and were demise chartered from Elka Shipping Ltd., London, for who they had been built as *Elka Nikolas*, *Elka Angelique*, and *Elka Eleftheria* respectively.

In recent years Royal Dutch Shell has being renewing its fleet via Project Silver, in which other companies have contracted orders for 50 Medium Range tankers with Hyundai Mipo for long term charter to Shell. All the vessels incorporate "Silver" in their names. The biggest participant in the programme has been Sinokor Merchant Marine of Seoul, previously known as a container ship company and the first to operate a container service between South Korea and China. Sinokor initially ordered 20 tankers from Hyundai Mipo in a contract worth about US$680m. The first, *Silver Ginny*, was delivered in 2014 followed by *Silver Valerie*. Sinokor eventually ordered 34 ships in total. The completions for Sinokor included perhaps the most interesting newbuildings in Project Silver -- a group which revived traditional Shell names. The first of these, *Silver Euplecta* and *Silver Ebalina*, were delivered in 2015 as the 26th and 27th 'Silver' ships, and were followed by *Silver Ervilia*, *Silver Eburna*, *Silver Entalina*, and *Silver Etrema* in 2016.

Ten 'Silvers' were ordered by Oman Shipping Co, with the first, *Muscat Silver* and *Rustaq Silver*, delivered in 2015. The Tristar Group of Dubai took six, all to be delivered in 2016, the first being *Silver Manoora*.

In a look at a history of what has been a large part of the Shell fleet, it is worth mentioning an interesting tradition, that of carrying a specimen of the shell from which the ship took its name, displayed in a case set into the bulkhead in the officers dining saloon. They looked good and made an interesting feature, and the case was usually internally lit, with a small plaque under it with details about that particular mollusc. Early stories said some of the shells were very valuable and needed guarding, but seafarers believed if that had been the case the company would have chosen a cheaper name.

When *Hyria* sailed to Kaohsiung for scrapping in 1975, Shell's list of requirements included sending the shell back, and the crew built a small but heavy wooden case for it. In the end the engineer superintendent just took it back in an envelope in his pocket. The shells ranged in size and some were so tiny a magnifying glass had to be mounted over them, often aboard VLCCs! Many names, like *Hygromia*, were difficult to pronounce and a challenge to send in the days of morse lamps. The practice of displaying a shell aboard did not extend to Shell's managed ships. Today the company manages a large number of LNG tankers for Qatar, with Arabic names, so they will not be carrying any shells.

A different role for a product tanker: Shell's H class *Halia* (1958/19,172dwt) helps lighten the 77,648 dwt *Pacific Glory* when the latter, carrying crude oil, was abandoned after a collision and fire off the Isle of Wight in October 1970. (Authors' collection)

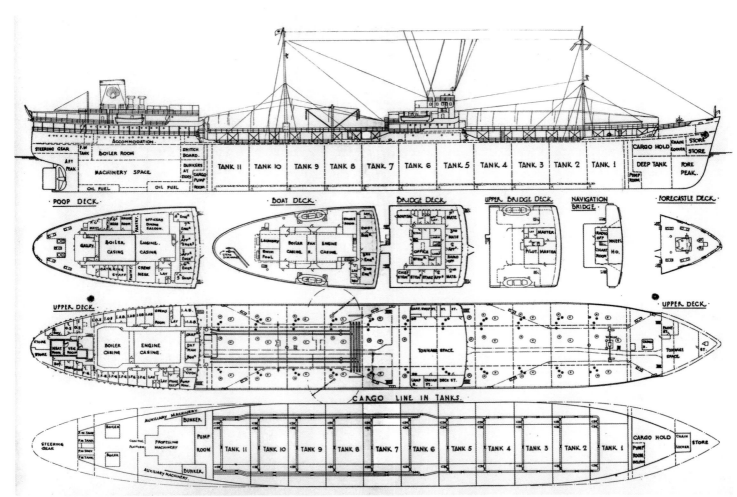

General arrangement drawings of *Hadra* of 1954, one of the large H and K class fleet of tankers that served Shell well for many years (top). "Blowing tubes" on another H class, *Hemisinus* of 1957 (centre). This was done daily at sea on steam vessels. (Shell Fleet Association)

Desmoulea **– Shell Petroleum Co, UK; Lithgows, Port Glasgow, 1939; 11,900 dwt, 147.21 m, Kincaid-B&W. (R Wilson/R A Priest collection)**

Tankers like the motorship *Desmoulea* of 1939 were the backbone of Shell's general purpose fleet in the immediate post-war years. One of a class of twenty 12,000 dwt ships ordered before the war, she survived being torpedoed in the eastern Mediterranean twice in 1941 and soldiered on to go to shipbreakers in Hong Kong in 1961.

Hemitrochus **– Shell Bermuda (Overseas) Ltd, UK; Cammell Laird, Birkenhead, 1959; 19,214 dwt, 170.57 m, 33 ta, 1 ha, 2x5 tn 2x3 tn & 4x1 tn der, 2 x Cammell Laird stm turbs 8250 shp, 14.5 kn. (Tolerton)**

The enormous building programme of H class steam tankers which started in 1953 revitalised the fleet. The last H class completion was *Hemitrochus* of 1959, built as *San Emiliano* one of the seven for Eagle Oil. Given her Shell name in 1965, she traded for Shell until she was despatched to Kaohsiung in 1977.

Hemisinus – Tanker Finance Ltd (Shell Tankers (UK)), Cammell Laird, Birkenhead, 1957; 19,266dwt, 169.40 m, 33 ta, 1ha, 3x5 tn 4x1 tn der, 2 Cammell Laird stm turbs 8250shp, 15.5kn. (D E Kirby/ R A Priest)

Fine views of two H class, *Hemisinus* (above) of 1957 and the famous 'Honeymoon Ship,' *Hinnites* of 1956. Both went to shipbreakers in 1976, the former at Kaohsiung and the latter at Inchon. The transition from buff funnels to red came around 1963, and the pecten had been added after World War Two.

Hinnites – Rebron Ltd (Shell Tankers (UK)), UK; Vickers-Armstrongs, Newcastle, 1956; 19,257 dwt, 169.40 m, 33 ta, 1 ha, 3x5 tn 4x1 tn der, 2 Vickers Armstrongs stm turbs 8250 shp, 14.5 kn. (Trevor Jones)

Hemiplecta – Shell Bermuda (Overseas) Ltd, UK; Cammell Laird, Birkenhead, 1955; 19,214 dwt, 169.35 m, 33 ta, 1 ha, 3x5 tn 4x1 tn der, 2 Cammell Laird stm turbs 8250 shp, 14.5 kn. (R Martin/R A Priest collection)

Hemiplecta (above) was another Merseyside completion, and *Haustrum* (below) a product of north-east shipbuilding. Fuel consumption for these steam vessels was about 50 tn a day. Both were disposed of in 1975 — the former, which spent several years on Australian coastal service in the 1960s and is pictured at Bell Bay, to shipbreakers in Pusan and the latter, whose vicissitudes included being damaged by rocket fire in the Saigon River in 1967 and a collision in fog in the English Channel in 1974, to Kaohsiung.

Haustrum – Shell Bermuda (Overseas) Ltd, UK; Hawthorn Leslie, Newcastle, 1954; 19,165 dwt, 169.37 m, 33 ta, 1 ha, 3x5 tn 4x1 tn der, 2 Hawthorn Leslie stm turbs 8250 shp, 14.5 kn. (J Mathieson/R A Priest collection)

Africa Shell – **African Coasters (Pty) Ltd, South Africa; Swan Hunter, Wallsend, 1956; 19,315 dwt, 169.40 m, 33 ta, 1 ha, 3x5 tn 4x1 tn der, 2 Wallsend Slipway stm turbs 8250 shp, 15.5kn. (Trevor Jones)**

Built as *Helisoma*, *Africa Shell* (above) took a new name in 1973 for South African coastal service, registered in Durban. Four years later she sailed on the familiar last passage for the Hs, to Kaohsiung. Also out of Africa is this shot of *Hadra* (below) at Cape Town. *Hadra* was yet another victim of the breakers' torches at Kaohsiung, in her case in 1975.

Hadra – **Shell Bermuda (Overseas) Ltd, UK; Smith's Dock, Middlesbrough, 1954; 19,149 dwt, 169.37m, 33 ta, 1 ha, 3x5 tn 4x1 tn der, 2 Hawthorn Leslie stm turbs 8250 shp, 14.5 kn. (Trevor Jones)**

A look inside the wheelhouse of the H class *Halia* of 1958 and a deck view of another H, *Hyala* of 1955. The navigating equipment layout of *Halia* was standard for the Hs, and basic but functional. Prominent are two radars, the 'periscope' for emergency magnetic compass above the wheel, helm and RPM indicators above the forward windows, the clear-view rotating window, the engine telegraph, a gyro repeater against forward bulkhead, and VHF radio sets just inside sliding wheelhouse door. For the watch the most important item was the bridge electric kettle, out of sight in the far corner!

The deck view of *Hyala* shows the cluttered appearance of the main deck, with numerous small tank hatches and Butterworth plates, the steam winch on deck with wires leading around various leads to the starboard derrick, manual tank valves, davits at the ship's side for the accommodation ladder, steam pipes running along the flying-bridge, and the staining of the deck with rust beneath the flying bridge. Note the 'bus stop' shelter on the flying bridge. The red steam-driven gas-freeing fan, with attached steam hoses, had been used to ventilate one of the cargo tanks, but with the job now completed it has been removed from the tank hatch, and lies on deck ready to be stowed away. Also to be noted are the wooden doors to the amidships accommodation, twin radar scanners on the monkey island, deck cargo pipelines leading to amidships cargo manifold pipes (to discharge to port or starboard), and the array of wire rigging supporting masts and running between masts. (both photos, Shell Fleet Association)

Kylix – Shell Tankers BV, Netherlands; Nederlandsche Dok, Amsterdam, 1955; 18,431 dwt, 169.40 m, 33 ta, 2 Werkspoor stm turbs 8250 shp, 14.5 kn. (Trevor Jones)

As well as the Hs, 16 ships were built from 1954 to 1957 for service under the Dutch flag, all with K names. The Ks included *Kylix* of 1955 (above) *Kosicia* of 1957 (below). The latter was actually launched at Cockerill-Ougree's Hoboken yard, Belgium in 1956, but she was completed in the Netherlands the following year. The former was scrapped in Spain in 1984 and the latter in Kaohsiung in 1977.

Kosicia – Shell Tankers BV, Netherlands; Wilton-Fijenoord, Schiedam, 1957; 19,350 dwt, 169.40 m, 33 ta, 2 Wilton-Fijenoord stm turbs 8259 shp, 14.5 kn. (K Barr/R A Priest collection)

Korenia **– Shell Tankers NV, Netherlands; Wilton-Fijenoord, Schiedam, 1955; 18,101 dwt, 169.39 m, 33 ta, 2 Werkspoor stm turbs 8704 shp & elec motors, 14.5 kn. (J Mathieson/R A Priest collection)**

Two more of the Dutch Ks – *Korenia* of 1955 from Wilton-Fijenoord (above), which was one of four turbo-electric Hs and Ks, and *Krebsia* of 1954 from P Smit (below). *Korenia* survived a collision in the Tagus River in 1962 and went to Kaohsiung 10 years later, and *Krebsia*, sold to Greek owners in 1973, arrived in Spain for demolition in 1984.

Krebsia **– Shell Tankers NV, Netherlands; P Smith Jun, Rotterdam, 1954; 18,184 dwt, 169.36 m, 33 ta, 2 Wilton-Fijenoord stm turbs 8250 shp, 14.5 kn. (R Wilson/R A Priest collection)**

Acavus – Tanker Finance Ltd (Shell Tankers (UK)), UK; Bremer Vulkan, Vegesack, 1958; 18,938 dwt, 170.34 m, 33 ta, 1 ha, 3x5 tn 2x1 tn der, 2 Brown Boveri stm turbs 7500 shp, 14.5 kn. (Trevor Jones)

The Shell fleet took another step forward with the introduction of the A class, a mix of steam and motor tankers. Although of the same dimensions as the Hs, their streamlining ensured there was no confusing them with their older sisters. The British As included *Acavus* of 1958 (above) and *Anadara* of 1959 (below). The former was sold in 1984 to be scrapped at Kaohsiung but the latter went to ship-breakers in Spain rather earlier in 1978.

Anadara – Tanker Finance Ltd (Shell Tankers (UK)), UK; Hawthorn Leslie, Newcastle, 1959; 19,623 dwt, 170.39 m, 33 ta, 1 ha, 1x5 tn der, 2 Hawthorn Leslie stm turbs 7500 shp, 14.5 kn. (World Ship Society)

Alinda – **Shell Bermuda (Overseas) Ltd, UK; Smith's Dock, Middlesbrough, 1959; 19,418 dwt, 170.39 m, 33 ta, 1ha, 1x5 tn der, 2 Hawthorn Leslie stm turbs 7500 shp, 15.5 kn. (Trevor Jones)**

As *San Ernesto* (and completed only two months after the last H class *San Emiliano*), the steam tanker *Alinda* (above) was the only A class built for Eagle Oil, and changed name in 1964. She was sold in 1983 and broken up at Karachi. *Acteon* of 1961 (below) was one of the Dutch-flag A's and a motorship.

Acteon – **Maats. tot Financiering van Bedrijfspanden NV, Netherlands; P Smit Jun, Rotterdam, 1961; 18,380 dwt, 170.42 m, 33 ta, 8750 bhp Smit-B&W, 14.25 kn. (Chris Howell collection)**

Fulgur – Citizens Trust Co (Shell Tankers BV), Liberia; Haugesund MV, Haugesund, 1974; 32,229 dwt, 170.69 m, 21 ta, 1x10 tn cr, 2 MAN 12,000 bhp, 16.5 kn. (Mike Pryce)

The eight-ship F class clean product tanker series starting with *Fulgur* of 1974 (above) marked overdue renewal in the Shell fleet. They were built in a £47 million order placed with Haugesund Mek. Verksted, Norway, which also included the similar Norwegian-flag *Fjordshell* of 1974, a dirty products tanker and the first vessel completed. The other eight were Liberian-flagged and all fitted with two MAN engines, the first medium-speed diesels adopted by Shell. The ships had no steam-raising plant. They were fitted with four electric cargo pumps each of which could draw from any of the 21 epoxy-painted cargo tanks, and each of 900 cu/m an hour capacity. A combined machinery and cargo controlroom was located on the first poop deck. *Ficus* (below) was a 1976 completion.

Ficus – United States Trust Co of New York, Trustee, Liberia; Haugesund MV, Haugesund, 1976; 32,229 dwt, 170.69 m, 21 ta, 2 MAN 12,000 bhp, 15.5 kn. (Don Meehan/Chris Howell collection)

Fossarina – United States Trust Co. of New York, Trustee (Shell Tankers BV), Liberia; Haugesund MV, Haugesund, 1976; 32,201 dwt, 170.69 m, 21 ta, 2 MAN 12,000 bhp, 15.5 kn. (Tolerton)

Fossarina of 1976 (above) was another of the F class. The F class were financed by American banks, which probably accounts for them being Liberian flagged. However, the crews were still British or Dutch as usual with Shell, although they had to apply for Liberian certificates of competency. After they were sold by Shell, many of the Fs found their way into the fledgling fleet of Singapore operator Ocean Tankers, today a major tanker company. These included *Ocean Onyx* (below), originally Shell's *Felipes* of 1975.

Ocean Onyx – Nan Hui Maritime Pte Ltd, Singapore; Haugesund MV, Haugesund, 1975; 32,229 dwt, 170.69 m, 24 ta, 2 MAN 12,000 bhp, 15.5 kn. (Tolerton)

Ervilia – Shell Tankers (UK) Ltd, UK; Mitsui Engineering & Shipbuilding, Chiba, Ichihara, 1979; 31,375 dwt, 170.01 m, 23 ta, 11,200 bhp Mitsui-B&W, 14 kn. (Tolerton)

Ten E class were built by St Johns Shipbuilding in Canada (six) and by Mitsui Engineering & Shipbuilding (four), and gave Shell lengthy and reliable service. *Ervilia* (above) was a Mitsui completion, as was *Ebalina* (below), which in this bow shot shows the impressive appearance of the Es with their towering accommodation and bridge block and the sturdy 10tn midships manifold crane and 5 tn stores and engine spare parts crane adjacent to the funnel that were a feature of the Mitsui quartet. The Canadian-built ships also had 10 tn hose-handling and 5tn stores cranes. Completed in 1979 and 1980 respectively and both British registered, *Ervila* was sold in 2000 and went to Alang in 2007, and *Ebalina* was sold in 1998 for US$5.6 million to become *Lampedusa* and went to Chittagong in 2007.

Ebalina – Shell Tankers (UK) Ltd, UK; Mitsui, Ichihara, 1980; 31,374 dwt, 170.01 m, 21 ta, 11,200 bhp Mitsui-B&W, 14.5 kn. (Tolerton)

Euplecta – Shell Tankers (UK) Ltd, UK; Mitsui, Ichihara, 1980; 31,374 dwt, 170.01 m, 21 ta, 11,200 bhp Mitsui-B&W, 14.5 kn. (Tolerton)

The British *Euplecta* (above) was one of the Mitsui quartet, while the German-managed, Liberian-flagged *Elona* (below) was Canadian-built. They are pictured with the red hulls first adopted by Shell after buying *Gerina*, renamed *Norrisia*, from Norwegian owners in 1987 for North Sea work. As *Gerina* she had red hull and decks, and Shell initially painted the hull black before later switching back to red. In 1989 after one of the periodic corporate re-imaging exercises, a new Danish-built Z class quartet emerged with red hulls and decks, and the rest of the fleet soon followed. *Euplecta* was sold in 2001 and *Elona* in 1996, and both were scrapped at Chittagong, arriving in 2009 and 2007 respectively.

Elona – Lepton Shipping Corp (Deutsche Shell Tanker GmbH), Liberia; Saint John Shipbuilding, St John NB, 1979; 31,487 dwt, 169.20 m, 21 ta, 12,000 bhp Cegielski-Sulzer, 14.5 kn. (Tolerton)

Hadra – Hubert Shipping Ltd (Shell International Shipping), Netherlands; Halla Engineering & HI, Inchon, 1994; 46,851 dwt, 183.20 m, 8 ta & 2 slop ta, 10,139 bhp Hyundai-B&W, 14.5 kn. (Tolerton)

Shell updated its product tanker fleet with six new 47,000 dwt H class ships completed in South Korea by Halla Engineering & Heavy Industries in 1993 and 1994. Shell's previous H class tankers of the 1950s had been 19,000 dwt vessels on an overall length only about 14 m less. The new Hs, which all revived names from the previous series, included *Hadra* (above) and *Haustrum* (below). The Halla H's had eight cargo tanks and two slop tanks with eight cargo pumps each of 850 cu/m an hour capacity. They were of course double-hulled, and also classified as "ice capable." All were delivered with red hulls and the red funnel with the Shell pecten.

Haustrum – Viken H Class Ltd (Shell International Trading & Shipping Co.), Isle of Man (UK); Halla, Inchon, 1994; 46,801 dwt, 183.20 m, 8 ta, 10,140 hp Hyundai-B&W, 14.5 kn. (Tolerton)

Haminea – Viken H Class Ltd (Shell International Trading & Shipping), Isle of Man (UK); Halla, Inchon, 1994; 46,851 dwt, 183.20 m, 8ta & 2 slop ta, 10,147 hp Hyundai-B&W, 14.5 kn. (Tolerton)

The new H class later discarded the red Shell livery for an unobtrusive colour scheme of black hulls and buff funnels with black tops (the original Anglo-Saxon fleet colours), as seen on *Haminea* (above) and *Hatasia* (below). All six Hs were all sold in 2006-07 and raised the Singapore ensign as part of the Tanker Pacific Management fleet. The new names were *Pacific Amber* (*Halia*), *Pacific Crystal* (*Hastula*), *Pacific Opal* (*Hatasia*), *Pacific Jade* (*Haustrum*), *Pacific Pearl* (*Hadra*), and *Pacific Ruby* (*Haminea*).

Hatasia – Viken H Class Ltd (Shell International Trading & Shipping), Isle of Man; Halla, Inchon, 1993; 46,851 dwt, 183.20 m, 8 ta & 2 slop ta, 10,147 hp Hyundai-B&W, 14.5 kn. (Tolerton)

Helix – **Phinda Pty Ltd, Australia; Stocznin Szczecinska, Szczecin, 1997; 46,092dwt, 182.96m, 20 ta & 2 slop ta, 12,018 hp Cegielski-Sulzer, 14.5 kn. (Tolerton)**

Old H class names were also revived for two tankers which were employed on the Australian coast by Shell, the 46,092dwt Polish-built *Helix* of 1997 (above), registered in the Victorian port of Geelong and a virtual sister of the New Zealand coastal tanker *Kakariki*, and the Douglas-registered 50,266 dwt chemical and products carrier *Helcion* of 2008 (below), built at SPP Shipbuilding in South Korea and launched as *Mexico*. *Helix* was sold in 2011 and has since traded as *Araluen Spirit* and, for two years in South African waters, as *Hippo* for Unicorn Lines, and latter was sold in 2011 to Teekay Shipping and renamed *Tandara Spirit*, but chartered back to Shell.

Helcion – **Energetic Tank Inc (STASCO Ship Management), Isle of Man (UK); SPP Shipbuilding, Tongyeong, 2008; 50,266 dwt, 183 m, 12 ta & 2 slop ta, 12,889 hp Doosan-MAN-B&W, 14.9 kn. (Tolerton)**

Ficus – Angelique Navigation Ltd (Shell International Trading & Shipping Co), Isle of Man (UK); Brodo-gradiliste 'Split,' Split, 2001; 44,788 dwt, 183.40 m, 16 ta, 12,480 bhp Tvornica-B&W, 16 kn. (Anton de Krieger)

Ficus (above) was one of three chemical-products tankers in a new F class built by Brodosplit in 2001 and chartered from Elka Shipping until 2009, when she reverted to the name she had when she was launched, *Elka Angelique*. The 12,887 dwt *Achatina* (below) is on a long-term bareboat charter by Shell to carry smaller product parcels. She was completed in 2005 as *Cape Essvik* along with her sister *Acavus* (*Cape Eden)* at Samho Shipbuilding, Tongyeong. They have 12 cargo tanks each with a 300 cu/m an hour pump. The similar sized *Arianta* completed by Bodewes Volharding, Foxhol, in 2004 and smaller *Asprella* from Frisian Shipyard Welgelegen, Harlingen, (2001) were also chartered by Shell for some years.

Achatina – Viken Fleet I AS (STASCO Ship Management), Isle of Man (UK); Samho Shipbuilding, Tongyeong, 2005; 12,887 dwt, 127.20 m, 12 ta & 2 slop ta, 7043 hp STX-MAN-B&W, 13.4 kn. (Tolerton)

British Cormorant -- **BP Tanker Co., UK; Harland & Wolff, Belfast, 1961; 16.259 dwt, 160.08 m, 27 ta, 8600 bhp Harland & Wolff, 14.5 kn. (Trevor Jones)**

A fine study of *British Cormorant* of 1961 (above), one of BP's 14 classic Bird class tankers. She was one of six of the class built by Harland & Wolff – three from Belfast, including *British Cormorant*, and three from Glasgow. Sold in 1977 as *Oriental Endeavour,* she finished her days in Thailand, a country not usually associated with shipbreaking, in 1983. The ill-fated River class *British Trent* of 1973 (below), on which nine lives were lost after a collision and fire in Flushing Roads in 1993. (WSS/Keith Byass)

British Trent – **BP Shipping Ltd, UK; Eriksbergs-Lindholmen, Göteborg, 1973; 25,147 dwt, 171.46 m, 14 ta, 2x5 tn cr, 9,000 bhp Eriksbergs-B&W, 15.5 kn. (WSS/Keith Byass)**

BP's Product Tankers

Few shipping companies suffered more grievously in World War Two than BP. The oil giant's shipping arm, British Tanker Co, had a fleet of 92 ships on the eve of the war. Fifty ships (six of them managed vessels) were lost during the war and 25 ships were damaged.

The redevelopment of the BP tanker fleet after World War Two included the purchase of 10 US-built T2 tankers in 1947, and in some respects provides an interesting comparison to its rival Shell. While Shell's rebuilding programme of general purpose ocean-going tankers got under way seriously with the steam-powered H class of the 1950s, BP was off the mark much earlier in its renewal.

Indeed the British Tanker Co's post-war construction programme was probably the most ambitious of any shipping company in the world. BP had wide experience with motor tankers after commissioning a class of 21 12,250 dwt vessels before the war. And it opted for motor tankers from the start in its postwar building programme, because of their more economic fuel consumption – although it meant having two Scotch boilers for the steam cargo pumps and auxiliary engine room pumps and equipment, which meant extra weight and more space required. The diesel engines also needed more maintenance.

British Chivalry completed by Blythswood Shipbuilding, Glasgow, in January 1949 and *British Fame* from Swan, Hunter & Wigham Richardson, Wallsend, in February 1949 were the first of a series of 16,800 dwt motor tankers of rather similar dimensions to the T2s, and the 20 vessels were completed at 10 British shipyards over an eight-year span. Swan, Hunter contributed six of them.

However, the primary emphasis immediately after the war was on the construction of a series of vessels of around 12,250 dwt, ships essentially similar to the class built just before the war.

No fewer than 57 of this size, all motorships, were built from *British Supremacy* of 1945 through to *British Maple* of 1951, and along with 10 small 8400 dwt tankers ensured BP was back to pre-war strength very quickly. As a quasi-national corporation, BP pointedly shared its orders around many different British yards in its construction programme of the 1940s and 50s, and nine shipyards contributed 12s for the company.

The overall length of the post-war 12s varied a little from the 147.52 m of the first two completions to 149.60 m, but nearly half of them were 149.35m. Beam varied from 18.11m of the first two to 18.97 m. Deadweight tonnage ranged from 12,120 to 12,560. Some including *British Scientist*, *Security*, *Advocate*, *Strength*, and *Ranger* did not have a forward pumproom, possibly because they were designated as black oil carriers.

While the 12s were built for worldwide trading, their size made them handy for small and confined ports. *British Craftsman* of 1951, for example, during December 1963 made two trips to Svolvaer in the Lofoten Islands, a tight squeeze for berthing. Some of the 12s were renamed with Clyde prefixes on transfer to the BP Clyde Tanker Co in 1957-58.

What seems the relatively small size today of the 12s did not prevent them being employed worldwide. *British Liberty* of 1949 from Doxford & Sons, for example, probably on her maiden voyage, discharged a cargo from BP's giant Abadan (Iran) refinery at Wellington, New Zealand, in July 1949 and then sailed again for Abadan. Reports noted that she had nine cargo tanks and two steam-driven cargo pumps, each capable of discharging 500 tons an hour, had a four cylinder opposed piston 3100bhp Doxford engine, and made 12.8kn laden on trial. The engine ran on Haifa heavy fuel instead of diesel oil, and this was proving "quite satisfactory."

Late in 1950, *British Workman*, a 1949 12 from Harland & Wolff's Glasgow yard, was also on the New Zealand coast to discharge motor spirit from Abadan at Wellington, Lyttelton, and Dunedin before sailing for Miri (Sarawak). The *Workman*, incidentally, is the subject of one of the tales that became a legend in BP: After a sly paint job by the work crew, she is said to have arrived at a UK port from the Middle East with *British Workhouse* emblazoned on her stern.

Essentially scaled up versions of the 12s, the 16s started with *British Chivalry* and *British Fame* which both entered service in 1949, and although the 'product' carrier term had not been coined the 16s were BP's product tanker mainstays of the 1950s, when the first 'supertankers,' modest ships though they were by the standards of just a decade or two later, were being built for the crude trade.

The 16s in order of completion were:

1949 — *British Chivalry* (Blythswood, Glasgow), *British Fame* (Swan Hunter, Wallsend), *British Resource* (Hawthorn Leslie, Newcastle).

1950 — *British Reliance* (Sir James Laing, Sunderland), *British Freedom* (Swan Hunter), *British Splendour* (Swan Hunter).

1951 — *British Sportsman* (Swan Hunter), *British Seafarer* (Hawthorn Leslie).

1953 — *British Flag* (Hawthorn Leslie), *British Oak* (Smith's Dock, Middlesbrough), *British Guardian* (Lithgows, Port Glasgow), *British Envoy* (Doxford, Sunderland).

1954 — *British Crusader* (Cammell Laird, Birkenhead), *British Hero* (Lithgows), British *Vision* (J L Thompson, Sunderland), *British Chancellor* (Blythswood), *British Patrol* (Swan Hunter).

1955 — *British Officer* (Wm Hamilton, Port Glasgow).

1957 — *British Renown* (Thompson), *British Vigilance* (Laing).

Deadweight tonnage varied from 15,800 to 16,672, while overall length was 166.72 m, beam 21.28 m, and summer draught around 9.14m. Most had 27 tanks in sets of three, and they had four horizontal duplex steam cargo pumps, two in each pumproom.

The six 16s completed in 1949 and 1950 differed from the subsequent vessels in having small monkey islands with radar huts prominent on them. The later ships had the monkey island deck extended over the bridge front giving them a distinctive brow, and side decks, giving a much larger deck area. In addition, improved radar on the later series eliminated the need for a radar hut to house the bulky earlier equipment. The last two in the series, the 1957 completions *British Renown* and *British Vigilance*, differed from the rest in having rather stubby streamlined funnels and square ports in the amidships accommodation.

Common to them all — and indeed their smaller sisters and also Shell's comparable tankers of this era — were the two tall very traditional masts which carried the wireless aerial and below it the triatic stay which supported the halyards for signal flags. Whether using Marconi or Siemens radio equipment, transmitting on the 'British' radio station system around the world meant the longer the aerial, the better the transmission and reception, although whip aerials were in use in less conservative fleets by then. BP's immediate post-war ships also hoisted their Suez Canal signal lights on the flag halyards, but the 16s and other ships from 1951 had a 'Christmas tree' stub mast to carry the lights required to make up the signals. Cynical old deck officers from Doxford-engined ships will tell you the triatic stay was also to support the 'Doxford house flag,' the two black balls signaling "not under command" when the engine was playing up again.

On the forward halyard was a distinctive triangle to which crew members attached the aerials for their personal radios, Eddystones, Pye Cambridges, and, for the lucky ones, Blaupunkt, to tune in to Voice of the Desert and Lourenco Marques for music and to the BBC World Service's Merchant Navy Programme.

The masts also supported the yardarms to carry the stays for hoisting the wind sails for gas freeing the tanks. By the mid-50s mechanical fans were taking over this function -- either water-driven Vent Axia 'Moaning Minnies' or compressed air-driven 'Screaming Abdabs.' Much more efficient, they meant a lot less work for the crew but were extremely noisy, and frequently turned off at 2000 hours.

British Vision boasted a new braking system for its Doxford engine developed by North Eastern Marine Engineering. In sea trials this reduced the time of stopping the vessel by more than two minutes.

During the 1950s, the 12s and the 16s were BP's main carriers in the product trades with both clean and black oils, but as with other 'general purpose' tankers of the immediate postwar era, they also carried crude cargoes. *British Resource* of 1949, for example, made the following voyages in her first 12 months:

Fresh water, Southampton for Gibraltar (a not uncommon fixture when tanks were still clean); crude, Bandar Mashur for La Plata; crude, Bandar Mashur for La Plata again; crude, Bandar Mashur for Swansea; crude, Bandar Mashur for Swansea again; dry dock, Falmouth; crude, Kuwait for Le Havre; crude, Abadan for Swansea; repairs, Falmouth; mixed, Swansea for Dakar.

Ten improved versions of the 16s were also built in 1953-56 for the Lowland Tanker Co, 50 per cent owned by BP with north-eastern tramp operator Common Bros and Hong Kong shipowners Matheson & Co having quarter interests. The 15,950 dwt *Border Regiment* from Scotts Shipbuilding, Greenock, was the first completion. Costing about 840,000 pounds each, they were distinctive ships with their tartan funnel band carrying the BP shield, and *Regiment* was followed by *Border Keep* (also 1953), *Border Lass, Border Hunter, Border Fusilier,* and *Border Minstrel* in 1954, *Border Reiver, Border Sentinel,* and *Border Laird* in 1955, and *Border Terrier* in 1956.

The 16s were also supplemented in 1954 by three 157.42m motor tankers, known as the 14s (although the deadweight varied from 13,712 to 13,829), from Harland & Wolff, *British Gunner* and *British Sergeant* from the Glasgow yard and *British Corporal* from Belfast.

The following record of *British Sergeant* over 14 months in 1959-60 gives a picture of some not untypical voyaging of a BP tanker running in the product trades at this time:

From Thameshaven to Punta Cardon (Venezuela); aviation spirit to Swansea; drydocked Falmouth; loaded Swansea for Avonmouth; Abadan for orders via Suez Canal on Christmas Day; loaded Abadan for Karachi; loaded Abadan for Karachi, Port Okha, and Kandla; loaded Abadan for Lourenco Marques and Beira; loaded Kwinana (Perth) for Auckland, Whangarei, and Dunedin; loaded Kwinana for Buenos Aires, via Cape Town for bunkers; Montevideo, for bunkers; Durban, for bunkers; loaded Abadan for Madras and Chittagong; loaded Bombay for Madras and Calcutta; loaded full cargo diesel oil Mina al Ahmadi for LEFO (Lands End, for orders); part-discharged Hamble, topped up Isle of Grain, discharged full cargo Grangemouth; tank cleaned on passage to Newcastle for dry docking. The crew was home just in time for Christmas!

This era also saw a change of name for BP's shipping arm to the BP Tanker Co in 1955. As the increasingly large specialist crude oil tankers were evolving, BP's product carriers of the late 50s were now carrying ever-increasing multi-parcel cargoes, often four and sometimes eight different grades. A BP deck officer of those days remembers a challenging lube oil cargo of eight grades which had to be loaded in a specific order at three ports for discharge at three ports. Among the consignments was nearly 2000 tons of transformer oil, which was purportedly approximately the same value per litre as whiskey.

The Doxford machinery that powered many of the ships brings mixed memories to old BP hands. A party piece for engineers was 'playing Doxfords' — lining up six engineers as the cylinders with their hands on their heads and another standing opposite as the engineer at the controls. More often than not a mate pretended to be the telegraph, making the appropriate 'dingling' noise. At the order 'Dead slow ahead' the control engineer would move his arms appropriate to starting the engine and the row of 'cylinders' would start bobbing up and down. All went well for a bit, stopping and starting astern, then eventually 'Full ahead' wrought total destruction with everyone collapsing in happy confusion.

BP's associate Lowland Tanker Co introduced an innovative new class in 1960 which seafarers on BP's own ships looked at somewhat enviously. As *Aluco* had done for Shell the previous year, this class of five motorships introduced the composite navigating bridge and accommodation aft, probably as a result of the familiarity of Common Bros, who managed the Lowland vessels, with this configuration on its ore carriers. There was even a trendy touch to the nomenclature, with a *Border Pele* among them. They cost about £1.66 m each, and the lead ship *Border Shepherd*, delivered by Lithgows in 1960, was 20,914 dwt, 174.35 m long, with beam of 22.26 m and 9.9m draught, and she was followed by *Border Castle* and *Border Pele* (both from Swan Hunter) and *Border Falcon* (Smith's Dock) in 1961, and *Border Chieftain* (Smith's Dock) in 1962.

As well as bringing a new profile, these ships had a 5 tn pneumatic crane for handling the hoses instead of masts or kingposts and winches, and this quickly showed itself to be an improvement. A streamlined signal mast on the superstructure incorporated two engineroom vents and a crosstrees to take the radar scanner and morse signal lights. There were also two 1tn cranes aft on the quarter deck and two 1.5tn cranes on the forecastle utilising the windlass for power, never used, for stores handling. The ships had 27 tanks, nine centre tanks each flanked by port and starboard wing tanks.

Less than two years after the last two 16s entered service came the first of the Bird class, *British Fulmar* of 1959. Also ships of around a relatively modest 16,000 dwt (significantly less than Shell's H class), the "birdy boats" are very fondly remembered by a generation of BP seafarers, and during 1959-62 BP completed 14 Bird class ships. Again, construction was shared around different British yards, eight of them.

The Birds marked a change from the earlier 16s with their streamlined appearance and the absence of the traditional tall masts. The accommodation was also greatly superior, and with the saloon aft stewards no longer had to stagger along the catwalk with food for the officers. However, the mechanical design, and tank, pipeline, and pumproom layout were the same as earlier ships, and the dimensions not too different. The improved accommodation added so much weight that the carrying capacity was reduced. To help offset this, the five 1961 and 1962 completions had a single mast forward instead of the goalpost mast of the earlier ships, and rails instead of bulwarks around the accommodation. These Marks IIs were also airconditioned throughout the accommodation, and had light grey (possibly fire-retardant) paneling in the accommodation, whereas the Marks 1s' cabins and public rooms were paneled in varnished sycamore.

The Bird class ships were:

1959 — *British Fulmar* (A Stephen, Glasgow), *British Trust* (Lithgows, laid down as *British Thrush*), *British Swift* (Scott's, Greenock), *British Gannet* (Blythswood).

1960 — *British Kiwi* (Smiths), *British Robin* (Lithgows), *British Gull* (Harland & Wolff, Glasgow), *British Mallard* (Harland & Wolff, Belfast), *British Curlew* (Stephen).

1961 — *British Cormorant* (H&W, Belfast).

1962 — *British Osprey* (H&W, Glasgow), *British Kestrel* (Wm Hamilton), *British Merlin* (H&W, Glasgow), *British Cygnet* (H&W, Belfast).

Again all motorships, their deadweight varied from 15,262 to 16,183. Overall length varied slightly from 159.91m to 160.24 m, and beam from 21.08 to 21.15 m, while they drew 9.1 m.

Like the 14s and 16s, the Bird class had direct loading lines to the No.2 centre and No.6 centre tanks, and additional separate suctions to allow two lots of about 600tns to be segregated. However, pumprooms and pipelines remained standard in the different classes, each pumproom having two steam-driven 500tn an hour horizontal duplex reciprocating cargo pumps coupling into the ring pipeline system. Each pumproom had two loading lines dropping down the wings, although with the Bird class vessels there were two direct loading lines port and starboard dropping down six wing tanks to join the ring mainline, avoiding the pumprooms when loading. Able to carry several different cargoes of refined products, the Birds were true product tankers, and as well as having four main cargo lines were equipped for stern discharging and possibly loading, too. The stern line was a standard provision through the 8s, 12s, 16s, Trees, '-itys', and Rivers, and essential when vessels Mediterranean-moored to discharge at places such as Ravenna, Svolvaer, and Gan Island (in the Maldives, where there was an RAF base). And, in a less environmentally-conscious era, it was also used to discharge all the tank washings.

They were part of the last hurrah for the classic 'three island' tankers with bridge amidships, and the Mark 1s had a chartroom and a radio room behind the wheelhouse and also an owner's stateroom and a pilot's cabin (used by the extra third mate when coasting) on this deck, the master's and navigating officers' and navigating apprentices' cabins on the deck below, and, one deck lower, the engineers' accommodation, officers' smokeroom opening out onto a deck aft, and Chief Steward's cabin. In the aft structure were the petty officers' and crew's accommodation, officers' saloon, crew saloon, and galley.

The *British Kestrel* introduced several innovations, including a new waste heat recovery system said to be the most advanced in a diesel-engined ship, a combined wheelhouse-chartroom which became standard on all new BP vessels, employment of alternating current, and rotary vane steering controlled from the bridge. She was the only AC-powered "Bird," but her steam-driven turbo alternator was not successful as it did not like the 'wet' steam produced by the boiler.

In the early 60s, all the Bird class boats were docked and underwent sandblasting and then had all their cargo tanks epoxy-coated. This meant the end of one of the least popular shipboard chores for deck hands and apprentices, 'tank digging' to remove the scale and sediment that accumulated in bare steel tanks. Buckets on a rope had to be lowered through the Butterworth cleaning hatches for the sludge to be shoveled up and deposited over the side. Often rewarded with a tot of rum after the job was done, it was especially important before cargoes like avtur (aviation turbine kerosene) were loaded, but some mates ordered tank digging on every trip. The epoxy tanks saved enormously on time spent cleaning and gas freeing with the attendant crew costs in overtime, not to mention the steel wastage from rust.

Only two years after the last Bird, *British Cygnet*, was completed in June 1962 came the first of the Tree class, *British Hazel*, and in just over 10 years from *Hazel* entering service in mid-1964 BP was to add 35 more products tankers, firstly with 13 ships of the 21,000 dwt Tree class, then six of the 24,000 dwt '-ity' class, and then 16 of the 25,600 dwt River class. All were motorships.

Unlike the Birds, the ships of these three classes had the nowadays familiar composite bridge and accommodation structure aft. Taken as a whole, the ships from this extensive building programme did not have notably long careers with BP. The 13 Trees, 11 completed in 1964-65 plus two built in Australia a few years later for Australian coastal trading, were largely sold out of the fleet in 1981-83, although *British Beech* stayed under BP management until 1992 and the Australian pair were sold in 1987 and 1989. The six '-itys' of 1968 and 1969 were all sold in the 1980s — three of them as early as 1981. (Incidentally, when the six '-ity' names were repeated for a 2004-05 series of ships, BP dubbed it the Virtue class, but this term was never used for the '60s vessels.) Of the 16 Rivers all completed in 1972-74, three were quickly sold in 1976 to the National Iranian Tanker Co, and six more sold out of the fleet during the 80s. In 1996 BP owned only five product carriers, evidently preferring to rely on chartered vessels.

The first Tree, *British Hazel* completed by Swan Hunter, Wallsend, in 1964, introduced innovations including automatic and remote control of the main engine, with torque and acceleration-limiting devices fitted. There was the novelty of manoeuvring from full ahead to full astern controlled by a single lever in the wheelhouse console, and a Chadburn printer automatically recording all the telegraph orders and bridge control movements and the telegraph reply lever position against a time base. The ship could carry several different parcels of products with her improved pumping and ring main systems. And instead of the traditional derricks, she had an electro-hydraulic crane for hose-handling and a smaller crane for handling stores and engineroom spares. BP colour-coded its pumps and lines red, yellow, blue, and green, but on *British Fern* the cargo pumps were named Matthew, Mark, Luke, and John, and on another Tree, reputedly, were John, Paul, George, and Ringo.

The dimensions of *British Hazel* were: 20,462 dwt; 171 m LOA; 22.48 m max. beam; 9.46 m draught. The ship had 33 tanks. Speed was 15 kn.

The Tree class ships were:

1964 — *British Hazel* (Swan Hunter), *British Hawthorn* (Hawthorn Leslie), *British Fern* (Lithgows), *British Beech* (Laing).

1965 — *British Holly* (Lithgows), *British Vine* (Harland & Wolff, Belfast), *British Willow* (Laing), *British Laurel* (Eriksberg, Gothenburg), *British Poplar* (Eriksberg), *British Ivy* (Lithgows), *British Maple* (Eriksberg).

1967 — *BP Endeavour* (NSW Govt. E&SB State Dockyard, Newcastle).

1968 — *BP Enterprise* (NSW Govt.).

The latter two were Australian-flag vessels.

The last survivor of the Tree class, *British Holly*, sold in 1983, did not go to the breakers until

2006. *British Beech* was afloat until 2002, although BP seafarers were not sorry when the company sold her. Recalls one deck officer: "Isn't it funny that the most unlikely vessel should serve almost the longest. She was built by Sir James Laing at Sunderland, but they must have had some 'makey-learny' types in the yard. I always remember and can instantly visualise a plate on the fore end which had had a porthole cut when the plate was upside down and then welded back once the mistake was realised. It would have been a foot above the deck. That class was the first with the double ring pipeline system, which was fantastic. But on the *Beech*...! I think we had a count up of the valves, 133, all with 32 turns open to close, and as a new ship all stiff as hell. It took two blokes each with a wheel key to open or shut a valve." It once took two men four hours to wash and 'set the lines' before loading. In the subsequent '-ity' and River classes almost all valves were hydraulic.

After building all its previous product tankers at British yards, BP had commissioned three of the Tree class from the Eriksbergs, Gothenburg. And evidently pleased with the Swedish shipbuilder's work and prices, the company ordered four of the six ships to the subsequent '-ity' class from Eriksbergs, with the other two orders going to Yugoslav builder Brodogradiliste.

The '-ity' class tankers were basically larger, de luxe versions of the Tree class, with innovations including bulbous bows, exhaust gas boilers, inert gas, and hydraulic valves. Perhaps not surprisingly, they were irreverently known by their crews as the 'Titty' class tankers.

Dimensions of the first completion, *British Liberty*, were:

24,000 dwt; 169.63 m LOA; 24.82 m max. beam; 9.55 m draught. She had 33 tanks, a 5-tn hose crane, and 6-tn and 5-tn derricks. Speed was 16 kn.

The completions to the '-ity' class were:

1968 — *British Liberty* (Eriksberg), *British Loyalty* (Eriksberg),

1969 — *British Security* (Eriksberg), *British Tenacity* (Eriksberg), *British Unity* (Brodogradiliste, Split), *British Fidelty* (Brodogradiliste).

Eriksbergs received another six orders for ships in the subsequent 25,600 dwt River class series, and four contracts were placed with Belgian shipbuilders, while five went to Scottish shipyards.

The first River completion was *British Dart* from Eriksbergs. Her dimensions were:

25,651 dwt; 171.46 m LOA; 25.05 m max. beam; 9.58 m draught. She had two 5 tn cranes and a 1-tn crane for stores. Speed was 15.5 kn.

The *Dart* is listed in the registers as having only 14 tanks, but the normal arrangement in the class was 22 – six centre tanks (two long and four shorter) and 16 wing tanks, with a pumproom immediately forward of the engineroom. In this were four steam turbine-driven centrifugal cargo pumps, each with a capacity of 750 tn an hour. There was a double ring main system with four discharging and loading pipes at the amidships manifold but also a stern loading and discharging line run along the starboard side of the accommodation block. A conspicuous new touch in the Rivers unlike their predecessor classes was, as per many contemporary vessels, a prominent conning position protruding forward of the front of the wheelhouse.

The River class completions were:

1972 — *British Dart* (Eriksberg), *British Avon* (Scotts).

1973 — *British Test* (Eriksberg), *British Humber* (Brodogradiliste), *British Tamar* (Boelwerf, Tamise), *British Kennet* (Scotts), *British Tay* (Eriksberg), *British Esk* (Boelwerf), *British Tweed* (Scotts), *British Trent* (Eriksberg), *British Forth* (Scotts).

1974 — *British Wye* (Eriksberg), *British Neath* (Cockerill, Hoboken), *British Severn* (Cockerill), *British Spey* (Lithgows), *British Fal* (Eriksberg).

Although of similar dimensions, the 24,827 dwt *British Humber*, which had 33 tanks, was not a sister to the other Rivers. It was believed that the Split yard, having built two of the '–itys', successfully tendered for a River but was unable to build the hull, and after legal wrangling it was agreed to build an '-ity'-style ship instead. She was sometimes known in the company as 'Humberity.'

As well as the BP Rivers, two ships of this type, *Kotuku* and *Kuaka* (both 1975), were built by Eriksbergs for New Zealand coastal service. They were no-frills versions without inert gas among other things, and had eight identically-sized centre tanks, whereas the BP ships had only six centre tanks with No's 2 and 5 being double size. *Kotuku*, carrying black, condensate, and clean oils, had heating coils.

The last Rivers were sold in the early 90s while *British Trent* was destroyed by fire with nine lives lost after a collision with the bulk carrier *Western Winner* in Flushing Roads in June 1993. In 1996 BP had an owned fleet of only 13 tankers, of which five were product carriers. The shipping company had had another change of name to BP Shipping in 1981.

The products fleet had been embellished with the addition of *BP Admiral* (1990), *BP Adventure* (1990), and *BP Argosy* (1991) – all later given the British prefix, and Bermudan-flagged – from Mitsubishi Heavy Industries, Nagasaki. They were 41,000 dwt ships, 176 m long with 30.8 m beam and 11.52m draught, and featured a new centralized control room set-up, with all operations – navigation in one control area, and machinery, cargo, and ballast in another -- normally carried out from the bridge. The trio had only eight cargo tanks, all fully epoxy-coated, plus 10 wing and two peak tanks for fully segregated ballast on a separate pumping system from the cargo lines. Four grades could be carried, with four computer-controlled steam turbine-driven pumps which could discharge 3200tn an hour. The ships were also fitted with an inert gas system and crude oil washing, and had a 10tn crane for hose-handling.

This century BP has established a close shipbuilding relationship with Hyundai Mipo Dockyard, and the three 'As' were sold in 2004 when the first ships of a major new investment by BP in its product fleet came into service. The first ship in a new Virtue class of 12 large range, double-hull ships was *British Tenacity* delivered in April 2004 by Hyundai Mipo, Ulsan. Her dimensions were: 46,803 dwt, 183 m overall, 32.22 m beam, and 12.20 m draught. Speed was 14.8 kn. Designated 'crude/oil products' tankers, *Tenacity* and her sisters are of the now mandatory double hull construction, and have 12 corrugated-construction, epoxy-coated cargo tanks with plain internal surfaces, mounted on stools, plus two slop tanks with their own pumps, and 12 hydraulically-driven submerged cargo pumps each of which can discharge 600 cubic metres an hour. The vessels are based on a Hyundai standard design but with the addition of a forecastle, linked to the superstructure by a traditional tanker catwalk, and fewer cargo tanks. They have a free fall lifeboat at the stern and can accommodate a crew of 28. Some of the later deliveries in the series were built to an Ice class with more powerful engines as BP anticipated increased Baltic trading as Russian oil exports increased.

Tenacity was followed by *British Security, British Loyalty, British Unity, British Fidelity, British Liberty*, and *British Integrity* later in 2004 and *British Chivalry, British Harmony, British Courtesy, British Serenity*, and *British Tranquility* in 2005, all from Hyundai Mipo, Ulsan, and registered in Douglas, Isle of Man.

In addition to the Virtues, BP also took delivery from Hyundai Mipo, Ulsan, of five medium range, double-hull E class tankers from 2003 to 2007. Designated 'chemical/products' tankers, they were built for trading in north-west Europe, the Mediterranean, and the USA. In order of delivery, they were *British Explorer* and *British Esteem* (2003), *British Ensign* and *British Envoy* (2006), and *British Emissary* (2007). *Esteem* and *Explorer* were 182.55 m ships and the other three 184 m, and deadweight varied from 36,713 to 37,651. *Ensign, Envoy*, and *Emissary* were completed under other names for Capital Ship Management of Piraeus and bareboat-chartered to BP.

In December 2013 BP announced it was returning to Hyundai Mipo with an order for 14 medium range product carriers, nine of 55,000 dwt to be delivered from January 2016 to July 2017 and five of 40,000 dwt to be delivered from September 2016 to March 2017. The order was worth US $573 m, with the smaller tankers reportedly priced at US$40m each, the 50,000-tonners to be delivered in 2016 at US $41m each, and the 2017 50,000 completions at US$42 m. *British Mariner*, the first ship from this order, was launched on December 4, 2015, and delivered in early 2016, followed by *British Navigator*. Both are 45,999dwt. Hyundai Mipo has established itself as the dominant builder of product tankers, taking orders, astonishingly, for no less than 133 in 2013.

A deck view of the 16,000 dwt class *British Seafarer* of 1951 (top left). The River class *British Wye* of 1974 in extreme weather (top right) (both David Barnes collection). An aerial view of the 16,000 dwt class *British Officer* of 1955 (lower left, R Wilson/R A Priest collection).

The Bird class *British Swift* of 1959 discharging drums of oil on the Indian coast (lower right, Bavid Barnes collection)

Deck views of two BP tankers from different eras – *British Industry* of 1927 and *British Humber* of 1973. Common to both are the catwalk and the hatches for accessing the cargo tanks, although removing the myriad of bolts securing the covers on the 1927 vessel must have been a time-consuming process. One of the cargo derricks of *British Industry* is prominent, while *British Humber* has two 5 tn cranes for hose handling, one of them prominent here. (photos, authors' collection & David Barnes)

British Explorer – British Tanker Co, UK; Harland & Wolff, Belfast, 1950; 12,243 dwt, 149.30 m, 3500 bhp H&W-B&W engine. (R Martin/R A Priest collection)

The motorships *British Explorer* of 1950 (above) and *British Triumph* of 1949 (below) were among the huge fleet of 12s built for BP after the war which gave the company yeoman service before larger and more sophisticated product tankers led to their exits from the fleet. *Explorer* was renamed *Clyde Explorer* in 1958 and broken up at Santander in 1964, a year after *Triumph* arrived at Faslane for demolition.

British Triumph – British Tanker Co., UK; Cammell Laird, Birkenhead, 1949; 12,245 dwt, 149.35 m, 3200 bhp H&W-B&W engine. (R Wilson/R A Priest collection)

British Sergeant – British Tanker Co., UK; Harland & Wolff, Glasgow, 1954; 13,712 dwt, 157.42 m, 27 ta, 4950 bhp H&W-B&W, 12 kn. (Trevor Jones)

British Sergeant (above) was one of three 14s delivered in 1954, supplementing the large class of 16s completed from 1949 to 1957. These included *British Officer* of 1955 (below). She was broken up in Spain in 1973, the year after *Sergeant* ended her days being dismantled at a Japanese steelworks. The 12s, 14s, and 16s were all motor tankers.

British Officer – British Tanker Co., UK; Wm Hamilton & Co, Port Glasgow, 1955; 15,839 dwt, 166.72 m, 25 ta, 6400 bhp Kincaid, 13.75 kn. (L Rex/R A Priest collection)

British Vigilance – Tanker Charter Co, UK; Sir James Laing & Sons, Sunderland, 1957; 16,672 dwt, 166.82 m, 30 ta, 6800 bhp Doxford, 13.75 kn. (J Mathieson/R A Priest collection)

The last of the 16s was *British Vigilance* of 1957 (above) from Sir James Laing's yard, Sunderland, concluding a busy building programme for this class which stretched back to 1949. Ten improved versions of the 16s were built in 1953-56 for the Lowland Tanker Co, which was half-owned by BP. The Lowland vessels, managed by Common Bros of Newcastle and all given 'Border' names, included *Border Lass* of 1954 (below) from Wm Doxford & Sons, Sunderland.

Border Lass – The Lowland Tanker Co. (Common Bros); Wm Doxford & Sons, Sunderland, 1954; 16,030 dwt, 166.72 m, 27ta, 1x5 tn 2x4 tn & 1x3 tn der, 7040 bhp Doxford, 13.75 kn. (Chris Howell collection)

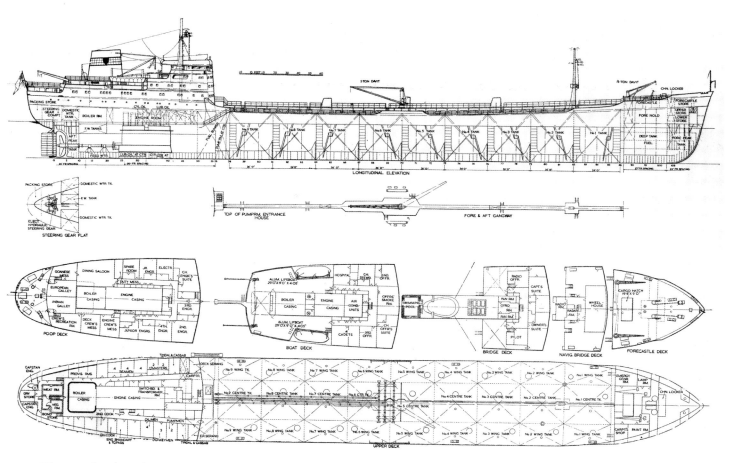

The Lowland Tanker Co. introduced a very innovative class with the five ships of the *Border Shepherd* series of 1960-62, with the navigating bridge and accommodation all aft. Illustrated above are the general arrangement plans for the lead ship (The Motor Ship). The photograph below shows *Border Falcon*, one of two ships built in this series by Smith's Dock, Middlesbrough, and one of three 1961 completions. She was sold in 1982 to Grimsby owner Ajax Marine as *Gardenia B*, but went to Kaohsiung for demolition only three years later. Fuel consumption was about 25 tn a day.

Border Falcon – **The Lowland Tanker Co (Common Bros); Smith's Dock, Middlesbrough, 1961; 19,949 dwt, 173.46 m, 27 ta, 1x5 tn 2x1.5 tn & 2x1 tn cr, 8000 bhp Hawthorn Leslie-Doxford, 13.5 kn. (K Barr/R A Priest collection)**

British Kiwi – BP Tanker Co, UK; Smith's Dock Co., Middlesbrough, 1960; 16,435dwt, 160.08 m, 27 ta, 8000 bhp Hawthorn Leslie-Doxford, 14.5 kn. (Trevor Jones, above, & R A Priest collection, below)

The 14 Bird class tankers built at eight different British yards are a group of ships very fondly remembered by old BP hands. One of them was *British Kiwi*, shown here in two quite different settings – arriving at Durban (above) and dressed (but in need of titivation with the paintbrushes) and at anchor at Eden, Twofold Bay, NSW (below). The grey hull as seen in the above photo was generally not popular with BP seafarers – and nor was the addition of the company logo to the cherished traditional BP funnel, although it was adopted a few years before the first 'Bird' went into service.

British Robin – BP Tanker Co, UK; Lithgows, Port Glasgow, 1960; 16,284 dwt, 160.18 m, 27 ta, 7500 bhp Kincaid-B&W, 14.75 kn. (Trevor Jones, above, & R A Priest collection, below)

Two different angles on another of the birds, *British Robin* of 1960 from Port Glasgow shipbuilder Lithgows. She is pictured as a rocking Robin in the swell off Durban (above) and at anchor at Wellington (below). She was sold in 1977.

British Curlew – BP Tanker Co., UK; A Stephen & Sons, Glasgow, 1960; 16,241 dwt, 159.92 m, 27 ta, 8750 bhp Stephen-Sulzer, 14.5 kn. (World Ship Society, above, & M Pryce collection, below)

British Curlew of 1960, pictured in her pomp (above), was thought to be the last Bird class tanker to be broken up. Sold by BP in 1976, the ship was damaged by shellfire in 1980 during the Iraq-Iran war while trading as Ocean Tramping's *Wenjiang*, and abandoned for many years. She ended up at Gadani Beach in 2011 (below) – a postscript to the history of one of the most famous tanker classes.

British Holly – **BP Thames Tanker Co, UK; Lithgows, Port Glasgow, 1965; 20,977 dwt, 171 m, 33 ta, 7500 bhp Kincaid-B&W, 14.5 kn. (Trevor Jones, above, & Dave Salisbury/Chris Howell collection, below)**

The 21,000 dwt Tree class marked a new phase of expansion, with *British Holly* (above and below in two contrasting views) among 13 completions and one of three from Lithgows. Her exceptionally long career was perhaps a tribute to her builders -- sold in 1983 to Italian owners as *Humanitas*, she sailed altogether under six names before going to breakers at Aliaga in 2006 as *Para*. She was the last of the Trees to be broken up. Fuel consumption of the Trees was 30.5 tn a day.

British Beech – BP Thames Tanker Co, UK; Sir James Laing & Sons, Sunderland, 1964; 21,093 dwt, 171.05 m, 33 ta, 7500 bhp H&W-B&W, 14.5 kn. (Don Meehan/Chris Howell collection)

Two more Trees in bloom: *British Beech* (above) and *British Fern* (below). They were among the first four Trees delivered in 1964 only two years after the last Birds were completed, and were larger, with more tanks, and a considerably more modern appearance. The *Beech*, which as mentioned earlier in this chapter was not the most popular appointment with BP seafarers, was sold in 1992 and went to Alang shipbreakers in 2002, and *Fern* was sold in 1983 and arrived at Aliaga in 1994 to be broken up.

British Fern – BP Tanker Co, UK; Lithgows, Port Glasgow, 1964; 20,977 dwt, 171 m, 33 ta, 7500 bhp Kincaid-B&W, 14.5 kn. (Don Meehan/Chris Howell collection)

British Avon – BP Thames Tanker Co. Ltd, UK; Scotts' SB Co. (1969) Ltd, Greenock, 1972; 25,620 dwt, 171.20 m, 22 ta, 2x5 tn & 1x1 tn cr, 9000 bhp Scotts-Sulzer, 15.5 kn. (Tolerton)

British Avon (above) of 1972 from Scotts at Greenock was the second River completed and something of a jinxed ship, suffering serious structural damage in the North Sea that nearly broke her back, and also a serious engineroom fire in the Gulf. She was sold in 1985 to Italian owners as *Mare di Kara* and after several changes of name scrapped in 2000 at Alang. Still unmistakably a River: The bulbous bow, projecting bridge front, and very elevated catwalk of the Rivers are well illustrated in the view above and the photo of *South Wind 1* (below), which until 1992 was *British Tay*. Swedish built, she was another of the Rivers to end her days at Alang, arriving in 1997.

South Wind 1 – TCP Marine Shipping Co, Panama; Eriksbergs (Lindholmen div), Gothenburg, 1973; 25,650 dwt, 171.46 m, 22 ta, 9000 bhp Eriksbergs-B&W, 14.8 kn. (Tolerton)

BP Energy – BP Shipping Ltd, Bahamas; Finnboda Varf, Stockholm, 1976; 32,265 dwt, 170.97 m, 20 ta, 2x5 tn der, 13,100 bhp B&W, 14.75 kn. (Tolerton)

Something of an orphan in the BP fleet was the 32,265 dwt *BP Energy* (above) which was built by Finnboda Varf, Stockholm, in 1976 for a Rethymnis & Kulukundis company as *Libra,* and acquired by the BP group in 1985 to operate under the Bahamas flag. She was sold in 1990. The *Energy* name was revived when a pair of chemical-products tankers, *British Enterprise* (below) and *British Energy,* were completed by Daedong Shipbuilding in 2001 along with the similar *British Endeavour* and *British Endurance* (both 2002) from Hyundai Mipo, apparently foreshadowing the Virtue series from Hyundai Mipo. The Daedong pair, which had a pump for each tank, was sold in 2006 to become *Green Star* and *Blue Star* respectively.

British Enterprise – New Star Shipping Ltd (BP Shipping), UK; Daedong Shipbuilding, Jinhae, 2001; 35,858 dwt, 183 m, 12 ta & 2 slop ta, 11,094 hp Hyundai-Sulzer, 14.2 kn. (Tolerton)

British Argosy – BP Shipping Ltd, Bermuda; Mitsubishi Heavy Industries, Nagasaki, 1991; 41,027 dwt, 176.20 m, 8 ta & 2 slop ta, 6300 bhp Mitsubishi, 14 kn. (Tolerton)

British Admiral, British Adventure, and *British Argosy* of 1990-91 from Mitsubishi bridged the product tankers built in the 1970s and the Virtues that entered the fleet from 2004. The trio went into service with 'BP' prefixes but these were changed to 'British' in 1993-94. *British Argosy* is illustrated above and *British Adventure* below. BP disposed of the trio in 2004 when the Virtues came into service. They had only eight cargo tanks, served by four pumps each of 800 cu/m an hour capacity. They were rather modestly powered, and fuel consumption was only 19 tn a day.

British Adventure – BP Shipping Ltd, Bermuda; Mitsubishi, Nagasaki, 1990; 41,035 dwt, 176.20 m, 8ta & 2 slop ta, 6300 bhp Mitsubishi, 14 kn. (Tolerton)

British Security – Logostar Ltd (BP Shipping), UK (Isle of Man); Hyundai Mipo, Ulsan, 2004; 46,803 dwt, 183 m, 12 ta & 2 slop ta, 12,870 hp Hyundai-B&W, 14.6 kn. (Tolerton)

The 12 ships of BP's Virtue class, completed in 2004-2005 by Hyundai Mipo, have been familiar in ports around the world in the past decade. *British Security* of 2004 (above) was the second of these 46,000 dwt tankers to enter service, and *British Unity* (below) soon followed her. Both have a pump for each of their 12 cargo tanks, each pump able to move 600 cu/m an hour.

British Unity – Pipton Ltd (BP Shipping), UK (Isle of Man); Hyundai Mipo, Ulsan, 2004; 46,803 dwt, 183.20 m, 12 ta & 2 slop ta, 12,870 hp Hyundai-B&W, 14.6 kn. (Tolerton)

British Fidelity – Speed Shipping Co Ltd (ASP Ship Management), UK (Isle of Man); Hyundai Mipo, Ulsan, 2004; 46,803 dwt, 183 m, 12 ta & 2 slop ta, 12,870 hp Hyundai-B&W, 14.6 kn. (Tolerton, above, & John Travis, below)

Two of the Virtues, *British Fidelity* (pictured above and below) and *British Loyalty*, both 2004 completions, were assigned that same year to Australian coastal service with Australian crews, the latter coming off charter in 2015 and being redeployed in BP's international trades, and the *Fidelity* in 2016 after loading a final cargo at Kwinana in February for discharge at three Tasmanian ports. The dramatic photo below shows *Fidelity* butting her way out of harbour in Wellington, New Zealand, in extreme weather.

The newest addition to the coastal fleet is the 183 m, 50,300 dwt *Matuku*, launched at SPP Shipbuilding's Sacheon yard on December 30, 2015. She replaces *Torea*, which has been on the New Zealand coast since 2007, and has been built for Silver Fern Shipping Ltd to be chartered to Coastal Oil Logistics Ltd, which schedules product deliveries and manages operational matters on behalf of its four shareholders – BP Oil NZ, Chevron NZ, Mobil Oil NZ, and Z Energy. The restriction posed by a bridge near the shipyard meant, as the illustrations show, that *Matuku* had to be floated out under it without her accommodation block installed. This and her bow thruster were fitted at another yard. (Photos, Jon Kelly)

New Zealand Coastal Tankers

With 14,000 km of coastline, New Zealand is more dependent than most countries on ships. For nearly 90 years hardworking coastal tankers dedicated to the trade have safely distributed oils and fuels around the ports of New Zealand. Since 2000 the service has been operated by Silver Fern Shipping Ltd, a division of the Melbourne-headquartered international ASP Ship Management Group. They have employed the product tankers *Kakariki* (46,724 dwt) and *Torea* (37,069 dwt), serving the ports of Auckland, Tauranga, Napier, New Plymouth, Wellington, Nelson, Lyttelton, Timaru, Dunedin, and Bluff, with each ship averaging 12 port calls a month. In September 2015 Silver Fern announced the pair would be replaced by two new vessels to be built in South Korea and chartered by Coastal Oil Logistics Ltd. The 50,300 dwt *Matuku*, built by SPP Shipbuilding, Sacheon, replaces *Torea* and entered service in 2016, and a 50,000 dwt tanker with bitumen-carrying capacity is due late in 2017 to replace *Kakariki*.

Until the construction of an oil refinery was completed at Marsden Point, Whangarei, in 1964, New Zealand was totally dependent on imported refined petroleum products, shipped in bulk by overseas tankers from the Persian Gulf, Singapore, Indonesia, United States or Curacao.

An early attempt to cover the distribution of the oil from the main ports in smaller quantities to the smaller New Zealand coastal ports was seen in the form of the case-oil carrier *Anamba* (1,835 gross tons, built 1902), which arrived at Wellington on April 9, 1926, from Singapore, via Lyttelton. *Anamba* had been purchased by Anglo-Saxon Petroleum Co, London, in 1910, for use in carrying case-oil to small ports in the Far East, and she was based for a short time in New Zealand. British Imperial Oil Co. Ltd (later to become Shell Oil New Zealand Ltd) had officially opened a bulk oil installation at Miramar, Wellington, on January 25, 1926. This was designed to receive and store oil products in bulk from tankers, then transfer them into drums, tins and cases (hence, of course, the term "case-oil") for local distribution. The employment of *Anamba,* which, with engines amidships, looked much like any other cargo ship, was only a stop-gap measure on the New Zealand coast until a purpose-built coastal tanker arrived.

This was *Paua*, built as Yard No.750G by Harland & Wolff Ltd at Govan, Glasgow, at a cost of £62,103, launched on April 14, 1927, and completed on June 9, 1927. (Because she followed the similar tankers *Petronella, Paula* and *Agatha* from the same yard [Yard Nos. 747G, 748G and 749G], she is frequently confused with them and reported as being a sister ship, but she was in fact a one-off design). Her delivery voyage began on July 9, 1927, when she left Southampton in ballast for Singapore via Suez. At Pulau Bukom, Singapore, she loaded 810 tons of petrol, then took 28 days to reach New Zealand, arriving at Bluff in a howling gale on September 11, 1927. She discharged at Bluff and Timaru before arriving empty at Wellington on September 16 to commence her coastal trading. Registered initially at London, her port of registry was changed to Wellington on arrival, and she became the first oil tanker to fly the New Zealand flag. Ship details were: 1,260 gross, 472 net tons, 217.3 ft. length overall, 36.6ft. beam and 15.1ft. depth. Her twin six-cylinder oil engines were of the 4S.C.SA type and were constructed by her builders; they generated 225 n.hp, giving a service speed of 10 knots. Specially built for the coastal trade, she had nine oil compartments, consisting of three centre tanks with a capacity of 804 tons of motor spirit and three port and starboard wing tanks holding another 273 tons, making a total of 1,077 tons. The tanks were also fitted with special tank hatches so that they could also be used to carry cased oil, and there was a forehold able to stow a further 2550 cases. For discharge of bulk oil, two cargo pumps with a capacity of 100 tons per hour each were used, and she was well equipped with derricks for handling the case oil.

Anamba was laid up for some weeks prior to *Paua*'s arrival, but a few days after her successor arrived she was manned with a Chinese crew, and returned to trading in the Singapore area. She was laid up in Singapore in February 1931 and was broken up in 1932, having earned her niche in New Zealand's coastal oil transport story.

Paua had her tank section renewed at Hong Kong late in 1939, and the opportunity was taken to lengthen her by 26 feet at the same time, giving her increased tonnages of 1412 gross and 620 net. She returned to service in January 1940 and traded around most of the New Zealand coastal ports, calling at Auckland, Tauranga, Gisborne, Napier, Wanganui, New Plymouth, Wellington, Picton, Nelson, Lyttelton, Oamaru, Timaru, Dunedin, and Bluff, carrying petrol and kerosene.

Her New Zealand registry was closed on December 15, 1950, when she was sold to Colon Shipping Co. of Hong Kong and renamed *Heather*, sailing from Wellington for the last time in January 1951. In 1954 she was sold to Pan Norse S.S.Co. (Wallem & Co., Hong Kong), and renamed *Lucky Carrier*. She went aground in heavy weather on May 30, 1956, about half a mile from Fakir Point, Akyab, (now Sittwe, Burma, now Myanmar) on a voyage from Chalna to Akyab in ballast. Refloated on August 8, 1956, she arrived at Singapore in tow on December 12, 1956. Declared a constructive total loss, she was sold and broken up in mid-1957 by The Hong Kong Chiap Hua Mfy. Co. (1947) Ltd.

Her replacement was *Tanea*, launched on May 17, 1950, and completed on July 25, 1950, by John Crown & Sons Ltd., Sunderland, Yard No. 231, at a cost of 297,024 pounds. Ship details were: 3060 gross, 1625 net tons and 3325 tons deadweight, 331ft. 10ins. length overall, 46ft. 1in. beam and 16ft. 8ins. draught. She was powered by a 4SA six-cylinder Werkspoor oil engine of 333n.hp made by Hawthorne Leslie & Co. Ltd., Newcastle. It gave a loaded service speed of 10.75 knots and burned 6.5 tons of fuel per day. Registered at Wellington, she had six sets of port, centre and starboard cargo tanks, with numbers 4-centre and 6-centre designed for the dual carriage of bulk oil or case oil. They were fitted with large removable gastight hatches, and flat metal guard plates were fitted to the internal pipelines to avoid damage by drummed cargo. Four two-ton derricks on the main mast served the two case oil tanks, and she had a trunk deck. *Tanea* was an almost identical sister ship to *Felipes*, which preceded her from the same builders as Yard No.230 and was delivered on 3rd March 1950 for Nederlandsche-Indies Tankstoomboot Mij., under the Dutch flag. The only external difference was the absence of derricks on *Felipes*'s mainmast.

The delivery voyage of the *Tanea* began when she sailed from Sunderland on July 27, 1950, and she came via Bari, Haifa, Port Said, Suez, Abadan, and Singapore. She arrived at Wellington on October 22, 1950, and took up the coastal voyages previously carried out by *Paua*, carrying only refined oils. Her trading around the New Zealand coast was mainly uneventful, one of the few minor incidents noted being her stranding in the Wanganui River whilst sailing in ballast from Castlecliff Wharf late in the evening of August 11, 1957. She was aground for only an hour and refloated after discharging 1000 tons of water ballast, but her owners were understandably anxious, as Anglo-Saxon had previously lost their case-oil ship *Cyrena* (2138 gross tons, built 1913) by stranding at Wanganui in May 1925.

The opening of New Zealand Refining Co.'s Marsden Point refinery at Whangarei early in 1964 completely changed the coastal distribution pattern, and *Tanea* became too small for the planned distribution of refined oils from the refinery around the coast. After drydocking in the floating dock at Wellington between March 31 and April 2, 1964, she sailed from Wellington for the last time on April 17, 1964, for Singapore. She had been transferred from Shell Co. of New Zealand and Wellington registry to Shell Tankers (U.K.) Ltd and London registry, for trading around the Singapore area.

In May 1965 she was working in South Vietnamese waters, and between July 1965 and July 1967 regularly traded from Singapore to Northwest Australian ports such as Port Hedland and Broome, sometimes calling at Cocos Island part-loaded on the return trip. Between July and September 1967 she underwent extensive steel renewals at Jurong drydock, Singapore, then between October 1967 and March 1968 served as a lightening tanker off South Vietnam. She then reverted to trading between Singapore and Northwest Australian ports until September 1968, after which she traded almost exclusively in the Singapore area. She normally loaded at Port Dickson, Pulau Bukom, and sometimes Miri, for discharge at Woodlands (Singapore Island), Kuching, Phuket, Penang, Telok Anson, and also made one-off voyages to Cocos Island, Nha Trang, Da Nang, Labuan, and Kota Kinabalu in 1969. From 1970 she traded exclusively between Pulau Bukom and Woodlands until she was laid up in the Western Anchorage, Singapore, on January 20, 1972. She arrived at Jurong, Singapore, on January 31, 1972, for demolition.

However, *Tanea* was followed in the New Zealand coastal trade by another tanker of similar size. She was *Maurea* (2928 gross tons, built 1952), which had been launched on November 28, 1951, and completed on April 4, 1952, by Smith's Dock Co, Middlesbrough, as *Fragum*, Yard No. 1219, at a cost of £333,771, for Anglo-Saxon Petroleum Co., and registered at London. Ship details were: 2926 gross, 1280 net tons, 3416 tons deadweight, 331ft. 11ins. length overall, 46ft. 4ins. beam and 17ft. draught. A triple-expansion engine of 1600i.hp gave her a service speed of 11.5 knots. Although of similar dimensions to *Tanea*, she was purpose-built to carry bitumen in six centre tanks, with ballast only in the wing tanks. She was mostly used in the West Coast of England trade, loading bitumen in the Mersey for Ardrossan, then sailing southwards in ballast to Heysham to load fuel oil for discharge at Mersey or Manchester Ship Canal ports, Belfast, or Dublin. *Fragum* was drydocked at Newcastle, England, towards the end of 1963 and was transferred to Shell Oil NZ Ltd and renamed *Maurea*, registered at Wellington. She was one of the first Shell tankers to receive the newly-modified funnel colours of red funnel with yellow shell. She arrived at Wellington on April 9, 1964, from Newcastle via Curacao and Panama, eight days before *Tanea* left for Singapore. *Maurea* started a new coastal trade of distributing bitumen and fuel oil from Marsden Point, while coastal distribution of refined products was done by larger overseas Shell or BP-owned or chartered tankers working around the coast (see below).

Maurea, however, was in turn to prove too small for the trade and was replaced by the larger tanker *Erne* in August 1970. After a period of lay-up at Lyttelton she was sold on April 17, 1971, to Ocean Bitumen Carriers Inc., part of the C.Y. Tung group of companies, and was renamed *Dayu*, registered at Monrovia. *Dayu* sailed from New Zealand for the Far East and changed her funnel markings to those of her new owners: blue with a black top, with a yellow star. She was next reported as working in the Saigon and Mekong Rivers, a trade for which her size would suit her admirably, probably loading cargo at Hong Kong or Singapore, or transhipping cargo from tankers at Saigon. Lloyd's List noted her as trading between Pulau Bukom, Penang and Port Dickson in December 1973. She was noted at anchor in Singapore's Western Anchorage on July 18, 1975. At a time of rising fuel oil prices her steam triple-expansion engines would not be very economical, and she arrived at Hong Kong in March 1976 for demolition by Fuji, Marden & Co. Ltd.

When Marsden Point refinery first came "on stream", the majority of refined products were carried around the coast by oil company owned or chartered ships. Thus, the first shipments of refined products loaded out of the refinery for delivery to other New Zealand ports were carried by the Dutch Shell tanker *Arca*, (12,222 gross tons, built 1959) and BP's *British Freedom*, (11,207 gross tons, built 1950). Such ships usually completed only a few voyages around the coast before being replaced by other similar tonnage. After a time, however, there came some local maritime union pressure to have local seafarers involved in the coastal trade on dedicated tankers. This resulted in a series of tankers being demise-chartered by the oil companies for operation around the New Zealand coast. They were operated under the management of the Union Steam Ship Co of NZ Ltd and were fully manned by New Zealand crew on New Zealand articles. They largely replaced the procession of overseas tankers that had previously been working the coast.

The first of these to arrive was *Athelviscount*, (12,778 gross tons, built 1961), initially chartered for six years and handed over to a New Zealand crew at Durban, first arriving at Wellington on

August 29, 1965. Owned by Athel Line Ltd. (of molasses tanker fame), she was completed in June 1961 by Smith's Dock Co. Ltd., South Bank, Middlesbrough, Yard No. 1261. Ship details were: 12,778 gross, 7322 net tons, 19,326 tons deadweight, 559ft. 3ins. length overall, 71ft. 7ins. beam and 30ft. 0ins draught. Single-screw geared steam turbines produced 7500 s.hp and gave a service speed of 14.5 knots. She had 11 centre tanks and nine sets of wing tanks, giving a total of 29 tanks in all. A pump room aft contained four 450-tons-per-hour centrifugal cargo pumps. Her original charter was extended and it was not until June 24, 1978, that she sailed from Marsden Point for the last time, bound for Hong Kong for scrapping. She arrived there on July 12. She was handed over to Shun Fung Ironworks Ltd. on July 22, and demolition work actually started on November 5, 1978. *Amokura* replaced her on the coast.

The second tanker chartered for New Zealand coastal trading was *Hamilton*, (13,186 gross tons, built 1960) which arrived at Marsden Point in July 1967 from Singapore on her delivery voyage after being chartered. Owned by A. Radcliffe S.S. Co. Ltd., and operated by Evan Thomas Radcliffe & Co. Ltd., she was completed in July 1960 by J Boel & Fils, Tamise, Yard No. 1364. Ship details were: 13,186 gross, 7804 net tons, 20,495 tons deadweight, 560ft. 0ins. length overall, 72ft. 0ins. beam and 30ft. 9ins. draught. A single screw 7800 b.h.p. 2 S.A. seven-cylinder Sulzer oil engine gave her a service speed of 15.5 knots. She had nine sets of port, centre and starboard cargo tanks, giving a total of 27 tanks in all. A pump room aft contained four 450-tons-per-hour centrifugal cargo pumps. Her registered owners were later the Hamilton Shipping Company, but she remained registered at London whilst named *Hamilton*. During her service of over eight years on the New Zealand coast, she made 321 voyages from Marsden Point (317 on the coast and four to Australia) and carried 5.8 million tonnes of products. She was replaced on the coast by *Kotuku* and made her last sailing from New Zealand on October 24, 1975, leaving Mount Maunganui for Singapore, where she was handed over to new owners, Feoso Oil Tanker S.A., Panama, and renamed *Feoso Sun*.

In November 1978 she arrived at Bataan Refinery, Manila Bay, and discharged 19,564 tonnes of Chinese crude oil. After discharge she anchored off the berth for survey to check for possible hull damage believed to have been sustained when she had berthed four days earlier. On November 8, 1978, while undergoing repairs, she exploded and sank at anchor, leaving her bows high in the air. Thirty of the 58 Chinese, Indonesian, and Filipino crew on board or nearby lost their lives, and many others suffered from burns. The wreck was sold to a salvage company for eventual scrapping.

The third tanker chartered was *Erne*, which was taken over by a New Zealand crew in July 1970, and carried a cargo of diesel from Singapore, arriving at Auckland on August 16, 1970. Owned initially by Nourse Line (James Nourse Ltd., London), management passed in May 1963 to Trident Tankers Ltd., in October 1965 to Hain-Nourse Ltd., in April 1969 back to Trident Tankers Ltd., and in August 1971 to P.&O. Bulk Shipping Division. She had been completed in February 1962, Yard No. 493, by Charles Connell & Co. Ltd., Glasgow, with details of: 14,244 gross, 8241 net tons, 20,090 tons tons deadweight, 559.8 ft. length overall, 71.9 ft. beam and 31.1 ft. draught. Single-screw with geared steam turbines of 8800 s.h.p., her service speed was 14.5 knots. She had nine sets of port, centre and starboard cargo tanks, giving a total of 27 tanks. Two pump rooms contained two vertical Duplex pumps in each. The after port one was later dedicated to bitumen. Just prior to entering on her New Zealand charter she went to Sembawang Shipyard in Singapore, where her numbers 4,5,6, and 7 centre tanks were converted to carry bitumen, and were fitted with extra heating coils for this cargo. An athwartship bulkhead dividing No. 7 centre tank, allowing smaller parcels of bitumen to be carried, was also fitted. Unlike the previous large tankers on charter, which carried refined white oil products such as petrol, kerosene and diesel, *Erne*, as stated above, replaced the much smaller *Maurea* as the black oil tanker, carrying bitumen, fuel oil, and marine diesel. She was to spend 14 years trading uneventfully around the coast, broken only by voyages to Japan, Singapore, Newcastle, or Brisbane for periodic drydocking and survey.

Her last sailing from New Zealand was on May 12, 1984, when she sailed from Bluff after discharging her last coastal cargo, arriving at Manila on May 28, 1984 for tank cleaning. On completion of cleaning she sailed from Manila on June 2, 1984, arrived at Kaohsiung on June 4, and berthed on

June 5 for demolition by Sing Cheng Yung Iron & Steel Co. Demolition work commenced on July 14, 1984.

Rather surprisingly, *Erne*'s 14-year stint on the New Zealand coast is not mentioned at all in the World Ship Society's publications on the P&O and Nourse Line fleets, although a photograph in the P&O book shows her with what became the standard funnel markings of all the New Zealand coastal tankers, a black funnel with a silver fern, which she acquired during her early years here. She was replaced on the coast by *Taiko* (see below).

During the mid-1970s increased output from the Marsden Point refinery required an increase in the coastal tanker tonnage available. Two new tankers were ordered which were virtually identical to BP's River class tankers, the main difference being increased accommodation space aft, gained by having the cabins on two decks built out to the full width of the superstructure block, instead of having outside alleyways as on the standard BP ships.

Kotuku was completed in September 1975 by Eriksbergs M/V A/B (Lindholmen Div.), Gothenburg, Yard No. 695, followed by *Kuaka* in November 1975, Yard No. 696. They were sister ships, with details of: 16,221 gross, 9954 net tons, 25,503 tonnes deadweight, 171.46 metres length overall, 25.02 metres beam and 9.57 metres draught. A single-screw 2SA six-cylinder B&W oil engine produced 12,500 b.hp and a service speed of 16 knots. They had eight sets of port, centre and starboard cargo tanks, making 24 in total, and the single pump room contained four 500-tonnes-per-hour centrifugal cargo pumps. An internal difference between the two was that *Kotuku* was fitted with heating coils in her cargo tanks to enable her to carry cargoes of black oil which required such heating to keep it fluid, but *Kuaka* was not so fitted.

Kotuku arrived at Marsden Point on her delivery voyage on October 30, 1975. *Kuaka* arrived at Marsden Point on January 25, 1976, from Sweden via UK, Singapore, and Miri, where she had loaded 25,500 tonnes of oil for the refinery. *Kotuku* replaced *Hamilton* in the coastal trade, but *Kuaka* was an extra ship. Wellington Tankers Ltd owned *Kotuku*, and Auckland Tankers Ltd owned *Kuaka*; both were part of the Papachristidis Group of companies. Both ships were registered at Wellington.

The next new arrival on the coast was *Amokura*, replacing *Athelviscount*, but she actually arrived at Marsden Point on July 22, 1978, from Singapore under her original name of *Hindustan*, and was renamed *Amokura* at an official ceremony in Wellington on August 8, 1978. She had been completed in September 1976 by Swan Hunter Shipbuilders Ltd., Readhead Shipyard, South Shields, Yard No.91, for Hindustan Steam Shipping Co. (Common Bros. [Management] Ltd.). Ship details were: 19,867 gross, 11,396 net tons, 32,240 tonnes deadweight, 191.98 metres length overall, 26.95 metres beam and 10.39 metres draught. A single screw seven-cylinder Sulzer oil engine produced 11,900bhp and gave a service speed of 15 knots. She had six sets of port, centre, and starboard cargo tanks, making 18 in total, and four 900-tonnes-per-hour centrifugal cargo pumps. She was owned by Marsden Point Tankers Ltd, also part of the Papachristidis Group, and registered at Wellington. Her sister ship *Kurdistan* in the Common Bros. fleet ran into ice and broke in half near the Cabot Strait in March 1979, her bow being sunk by gunfire, but the stern was later salvaged and a new bow built on. The incident of her sister ship breaking in half was not forgotten by the crew of *Amokura*!

As with previous tankers on the coast, the above three were demise-chartered to the oil companies and manned and managed by Union Steam Ship Co of NZ Ltd. Towards the end of their charter period, ownership of *Kuaka*, *Kotuku*, and *Amokura* passed from the Papachristidis Group to Ship Finance Ltd.

Amokura was sold during February 1993 and handed over to new owners at Botany Bay, Australia, becoming the Cypriot-flag *Transporter L.T.* During 1998 she was renamed *Eastman Spirit*. She sailed from Fujairah (Gulf of Oman) Anchorage on July 9, 1999, and arrived at Apapa (Lagos) on August 6. By September she had sailed to San Lorenzo, Argentina, from where she sailed for India. Later, while bound from San Lorenzo to Bahia Blanca (Argentina) with approximately 24,000 tonnes of vegetable oil, she grounded in the River Parana (Uruguay) on February 17, 2000, and obstructed the main channel. She was refloated with tug assistance on February 18 and continued on her voyage to Bahia Blanca, with no damage reported. She was renamed *Global Spirit* in December 2002, *Global*

Spirit III in May 2006, and *Northsea* in June 2006, and then sold to Indian shipbreakers. Although demolition was reported to have commenced on January 5, 2007, she was reported in distress on May 29 off the coast of Benin, apparently struck by lightning while in ballast awaiting orders. There was an explosion and fire, and seven of her crew of 29 perished. She was flying the Cambodian flag at the time.

Kuaka was sold on March 8, 1996, for $3.7 million to International Tanking Ltd, Bangkok, and made her last voyage around the New Zealand coast in late March 1996. She sailed from Napier on March 26, 1996, for Australia and Singapore. During her service on the coast she had completed 750 coastal voyages and loaded 250 feedstock cargoes from Port Taranaki, totalling about 25 million tonnes coastwise. She also made about 40 laden trans-Tasman voyages. She was handed over to new owners at Singapore on May 3, 1996, and was renamed *Sea Topaz*. Managers were listed as Rim Pacific Ltd. In March 1997 she was reported resold to Singapore interests for $3.8 million, and renamed *Trust A*. She was trading in the Mediterranean in September 2000. Registered owners were Ancora Investment Trust Inc, Athens, and she was Maltese-flag. In 2002 she was scrapped at Alang as *Sea Trust*.

Kotuku was sold on September 14, 1998, to European owners for $2.75 million, with delivery in late October 1998 at Brisbane, where she was renamed *Cercina*, under the Tunisian flag. She later sailed from Augusta, Sicily, on January 19, 2000, for La Goulette (north of Tunis), and she was trading in the Mediterranean in September 2000. Her registered owners were Compagnie Genérale Maritime, Suresnes Cedex. She was sold again to become *Bora* in 2003 and renamed *Bora 1* later that year. In 2010 she was sold for demolition and arrived at Gadani Beach on September 27.

To replace the bitumen carrier *Erne*, a new black oil tanker had been specially built in 1984. *Taiko* was completed in May 1984 by Mitsubishi Heavy Industries Ltd, Nagasaki, Yard No. 1920. Ship details were: 21,187 gross, 9327 net tons, 33,374 tonnes deadweight, 174.86 metres length overall, 28.05 metres beam and 10.6 metres draught. She had been launched as *Tara* but was renamed before completion. Actually owned by Union Steam Ship Co. Ltd., she was registered at Wellington on May 30, 1984. Initial crew industrial problems resulted in her being re-registered in Hong Kong on June 29, 1984, and she was operated by a Hong Kong crew for a few months, sailing from Japan for China, Guam and Singapore. She made her first New Zealand arrival at Auckland on October 2, 1984, and made a few coastal voyages before her registry was changed back to Wellington on October 9, 1984.

Australian Spirit was purchased in 1996 as a replacement for *Kuaka*. She had been completed in March 1987 by Mitsubishi Heavy Industries Ltd., Nagasaki, Yard No. 1985, for BP Australia Ltd., and was managed by Associated Steamships Pty. Ltd. in the Australian coastal trade. Ship details were: 23,547 gross, 8448 net tons, 32,605 tonnes deadweight, 182.4 metres length overall, 26.83 metres beam, 10.526 metres draught. She was renamed *Toanui*, and registered at Wellington as owned by Seabird Ltd., Auckland.

Toanui made her first arrival in New Zealand on January 4, 1996, at Tauranga from Kwinana (Western Australia). She also introduced new modified funnel colours. The familiar markings of black funnel with a white fern were retained, but with the addition at the base of the funnel of a horizontal white band with a narrower pale blue-grey horizontal band above it.

A new double-hull tanker for the New Zealand coastal trade was ordered on September 18, 1996, from the Sczecin shipyard, Poland. Her keel was laid on June 23, 1998, and she was launched on September 26, 1998, after which she was berthed alongside while the pipework, accommodation, engineroom, and electricals were fitted out. Hull No. B573-V, she was formally named *Kakariki* on December 19, 1998, by New Zealand businesswoman Judith Hanratty, company secretary for BP (a historical connection was that her father was marine manager for Shell New Zealand in the 1940s and 1950s). *Kakariki* performed sea trials between January 9 and 14, 1999, completed outfitting at the yard, and was handed over to Penagree Ltd., her registered owners, on February 8, 1999, registered at Wellington.

Her first voyage started on February 9, 1999, when she sailed from her builder's yard. She arrived at Ventspils (Lithuania) on February 11 to load a cargo of some 40,000 tonnes of diesel, and sailed on February 12. The diesel was for discharge at two ports in France, Donges, where she arrived on February 20, 1999, and Brest, where she arrived on February 23. Thereafter she sailed to Eleusis, a port near Athens, where she arrived on March 4 and loaded about 32,000 tonnes of naphtha for discharge in Japan/South Korea. She sailed from Eleusis on March 6 and arrived at Chiba, Japan, on April 4 and was transferred to the management of Silver Fern Shipping Ltd on April 7. She sailed from Chiba on April 8 for Singapore, where she loaded an oil cargo for Botany Bay, NSW, where she arrived on May 5, 1999. For the next month thereafter she traded between Australian ports. She arrived in New Zealand for the first time, at Lyttelton from Geelong, on June 8, 1999, then discharged at Wellington on June 9 before returning to Geelong to reload.

Ship details were: 27,795 gross, 13,258 net tons, 46,724 tonnes deadweight, 183.0 metres length overall, 32.2 metres beam and 12.92 metres draught. She had 22 fully-coated cargo tanks, basically 10 sets divided into port and starboard tanks, with the special bitumen tanks amidships further subdivided. She could carry up to nine fully segregated products, each discharged by deepwell cargo pumps fitted into her tanks. She had a complete double hull, with segregated water ballast able to be carried in the double-bottom and wing ballast tanks. She was also able to carry 3000 tonnes of bitumen.

In mid-1998 Coastal Tankers Ltd. (who managed and co-ordinated the tanker movements on behalf of the four oil companies – see below) reviewed their fleet requirements. They decided that with their larger ships, they could operate with only two tankers in the fleet, the new *Kakariki* and *Toanui*, and without a dedicated black oil tanker. Thus the intention was that *Taiko*'s charter from the Union Company was to be allowed to lapse in August 1998, and she was to be sold by them. In order to supply bitumen around the coast, it was planned to install an 1800 tonnes-capacity deck tank in *Toanui* to carry this product. However, this plan was further revised and eventually it was decided to retain *Taiko* on charter for the time being, and to sell *Toanui* instead.

At the end of July 1999, when the term of her original charter expired, *Taiko* was purchased from Union Shipping Ltd (as the Union Steam Ship Co had by then become) by the consortium of oil companies which had previously chartered her, and she continued to trade in New Zealand under the management of Coastal Tankers Ltd and Silver Fern Shipping Ltd. Her registered owner became Penagree 2 Ltd. She was sold in April 2007 and renamed *Atlantia*, and arrived at Alang on August 7, 2012, to be broken up.

Toanui sailed from New Plymouth on September 18, 1999, with a cargo of naphtha for Anjer, in Sunda Strait, west of Djakarta. After a period trading in the Far East, she was sold to Societa Esercizio Rimorchi e Salvataggi S.r.l. of Italy and was handed over at Singapore on December 21, 1999. After being renamed *Lorenza* under the Maltese flag, she sailed from Singapore bound for the Arabian Gulf. However, in April 2000 her new owners sold her yet again to Ultramar and she was renamed *Andoas*, operated by Petro Peru under the Panamanian flag. In September 2000 she sailed from Venezuela to Talara, Peru. Her name was shortened to *Ando* for her voyage to breakers at Chittagong, where she was beached on May 19, 2012.

In 2007, the South Africa-owned tanker *Nyathi* was chartered, and after a few voyages around the coast, was renamed *Torea*. A 15 kn chemical-products tanker completecd at the ShinA Shipbuilding Co yard in Tongyeong, South Korea, in 2004, she is of 37,069 dwt, and 175.90 m length overall, with 31.03 m beam. She is owned by Nyathi Ltd and managed by Silver Fern Shipping Ltd. Her cargo is carried in 12 tanks, each fitted with a pump of 500 cu/m an hour capacity, and she has two slop tanks. The engine is an 11,665hp B&W from Doosan Engine Co consuming 35tn a day, and manoeuvrability is assisted by a bow thruster.

In 2009 there was another addition to the coastal tanker fleet when the new 3900 dwt double-hull bunkering tanker *Awanuia* arrived at Auckland, intended to load heavy fuel oil at Marsden Point and take it to Auckland to bunker commercial shipping there, either alongside the berth or at anchor. Built in the inland city of Tuzla, Bosnia, she is owned by SeaFuels Ltd and managed by PB

Sea-Tow (NZ) Ltd.

The tankers in service on the coast have all continued a nomenclature inadvertently started by *Erne*, which was actually named after a river and lough in Northern Ireland. "*Erne*" was also the name of the white-tailed sea eagle, but its use has long since fallen into disuse. When the later tankers were built or renamed for coastal trading, they were given the Maori name of various birds. Thus *Amokura* is the red-tailed tropic-bird, *Kotuku* the white heron, *Kuaka* the blue heron, *Taiko* the black petrel, *Toanui* the shearwater, *Kakariki* the green parrot, *Torea* the pied oystercatcher, and *Matuku* the South Pacific reef heron. The coastal tankers load mostly at Marsden Point and discharge at Auckland, Tauranga, Gisborne, Napier, Wellington, New Plymouth, Nelson, Lyttelton, Timaru, Dunedin and Bluff. They also load condensate at New Plymouth for discharge at Marsden Point. They were managed by Union Steam Ship Co Ltd on behalf of the four oil companies (Shell, BP, Mobil and Caltex) until 1993, when management passed to Coastal Tankers Ltd.

Coastal Tankers Ltd had originally evolved about 1993 from the Coastal Co-ordinating Committee (known on the coastal tankers and to Union Company staff as "CoCo"), which, as its name suggested, co-ordinated the coastal oil cargo movements on the coastal tankers on behalf of the four oil companies.

During 1994, management of the coastal tankers passed from Union Steam Ship Co of New Zealand Ltd to Howard Smith Ship Management (New Zealand) Ltd. However, a short time after this, Howard Smith withdrew from shipping, and the management company re-emerged as Silver Fern Shipping Ltd. Coastal Tankers Ltd was wound up on October 1, 2000, and Silver Fern Shipping Ltd then assumed the role previously carried out by Coastal Tankers Ltd.

A different type of tanker to enter service on the New Zealand coast was the liquefied petroleum gas (LPG) tanker *Tarihiko*, completed in February 1984 by Ferguson-Ailsa Ltd., Troon, Yard No.559. Ship details were: 2169 gross, 650 net tons, 1872 tonnes deadweight, 81.11 metres length overall, 13.92 metres beam, and 4.88 metres draught. She was owned by Ship Leasing (1982) Ltd., operated by Liquigas, Wellington, and was managed by Blueport ACT, Wellington, until 1991, when management passed to P&O (NZ). *Tarihiko* loaded LPG at New Plymouth and distributed it to Lyttelton, Dunedin, and Onehunga. She played an important part in the rescue of passengers from the stricken Russian cruise liner *Mikhail Lermontov* in Port Gore on February 16, 1986, and took 356 souls on board. She was withdrawn from service and laid up at Dunedin during January 1999, and was replaced by chartered overseas LPG tankers. *Tarihiko* was renamed *Kilgas Centurion* on July 8, 1999, and transferred to the Singaporean flag, having been bought by Danish owners KIL Shipping, an associate of Knud I Larsen A/S. She sailed from Dunedin under her new name on July 10, 1999, with a Latvian crew, bound initially for Singapore, before continuing on to Europe, where she was trading in September 2000. On February 15, 2001, she ran aground on a sandy beach while on a loaded voyage from Teesport to the Thames, and was refloated undamaged by tugs the following day.

The tanker *Ellida* was purchased for US$9.6 million in February 1995 for conversion at Singapore into a FPSO (Floating Production, Storage, Offloading) unit. She had been built in 1976 by Nippon Kokan KK at the Tsunumi Yard, Yokohama, and was launched as *Vincenzia*, but was completed as *Umm Shaif*. Ship details were: 71,283 gross tons, 137,684 tonnes deadweight, 266.0 metres length overall, 43.578 metres beam and 17.02 metres draught. She was sold in 1990 to Morten Werrings Rederi, Norway, and renamed *Ellida*.

Renamed *Whakaaropai*, she was registered as a New Zealand ship at Timaru on 3rd May 1996 for the delivery voyage from Singapore to New Zealand. She arrived at her planned position offshore from the Taranaki coast on August 4, 1996, and was finally connected to her pre-laid mooring system over the Maui oilfield on August 13, 1996. Testing and commissioning of equipment was completed, and the first cargo off-loaded was on August 24, 1996, by the tanker *Pacific Onyx*. The commissioning of the FPSO ended a three-year programme which began following the discovery of oil in the Maui field in 1993. The field had an initially-expected life of four-and-a-half years, but additional oil discoveries have extended this.

Whakaaropai completed her charter in 2006, and sailed to Singapore under her own power. Next to arrive was *Umaroa* in 2007 at the offshore Tui oilfield, followed by *Raroa* in 2008 for the offshore Maari oilfield.

("FPSO" is a Floating Production, Storage, Offloading tanker. Permanently moored offshore, product from the Maui field is pumped into her through a permanent pipeline and stored in her until tankers come to load it from her into their tanks and take it away. Whakaaropai exported product for Fletcher Energy, whereas condensate loaded at New Plymouth is destined for refining at Marsden Point).

A dramatic view of *Torea*, in service on the New Zealand coast from 2007 to 2016, in boisterous weather (above). And a historic moment (below) as the coastal tankers *Athelviscount* and *Erne* pass in Auckland harbour on the former's last visit to this port in 1978. They are still a well-remembered pair -- the former was employed on the New Zealand coast for 13 years and the latter for 14. (Both photos, Chris Howell)

The little *Paua* (above), built at a cost of £62,000 as one of the more modest completions from Harland & Wolff's Govan yard, was New Zealand's first coastal bulk oil tanker and gave yeoman service from her arrival in 1927 until she was sold East in December 1950. The historic Lyttelton view (below) in January 1951 shows the *Paua* (left) under her new name *Heather* ready to sail for the East, with the interisland ferry *Rangatira* and dredge *Tewhaka* on the other side of the wharf. (top, Mike Pryce collection; bottom NZ Railway & Locomotive Society)

Tanea – Shell Co. of New Zealand Ltd, New Zealand; J Crown & Sons, Sunderland, 1950; 3325 dwt, 101.11 m, Hawthorn Leslie-Werkspoor. (Keith Wood collection)

The larger _Tanea_, a motor tanker newly completed at a Sunderland shipyard, took over from _Paua_ in 1950 as New Zealand's coastal tanker and was employed on the coast until 1964. In this attractive view taken subsequently when she was operating for Shell in the East, she is seen off Penang sailing for Shell's depot at Butterworth with her Malaysian courtesy flag visible.

Maurea – Shell Oil NZ Ltd, New Zealand; Smith's Dock, Middlesbrough, 1952; 3416 dwt, 101.19 m, 18 ta, 1x3 tn 2x1.5 tn der, 1800 ihp Smith's Dock triple exp stm, 11kn. (Mike Pryce collection)

The triple expansion steam tanker _Maurea_, built in 1952 as _Fragum_ and a similar sized ship to _Tanea_, took over in 1964, but it was quickly apparent the coastal trade now needed larger vessels. She was sold in 1971 to a C Y Tung company after a long lay-up at Lyttelton.

Athelviscount **– Tankers Ltd (Athel Line), UK; Smith's Dock, Middlesbrough, 1961; 20,492 dwt, 170.47 m, 29 ta, 2x5 tn cr, 1x5 tn der, 2 Hawthorn Leslie stm turbs7500 shp, 14.5 kn. (Chris Howell)**

The first of three tankers chartered from UK companies in the years after the Marsden Point refinery in Northland came on stream and manned by New Zealand crews, the steam tanker *Athelviscount* was owned by Tate & Lyle's Athel Line, the specialist molasses carrier. However, *Athelviscount* had been designed to carry oil parcel cargoes, signaling a move by Athel into these trades. She was on the New Zealand coast from 1965 to 1978 and is pictured on her last Auckland call.

Hamilton **– Anthony Radcliffe SS Co (Evan Thomas Radcliffe & Co), UK; J Boel & Fils, Tamise, 1960; 20,495 dwt, 170.69 m, 27 ta, 4x5 tn der, 9100 bhp De Schelde-Sulzer, 15.5 kn. (Tolerton)**

Hamilton arrived in 1967 and spent more than eight years on the coast. Completed in Belgium by Boelwerf in 1960 for Cardiff tramp ship owner Evan Thomas Radcliffe, she was one of a number of Radcliffe ships over the years with '-ton' suffixes to their names instead of Radcliffe's more usual 'Llan-' prefix, and the name had no connection with the New Zealand city of Hamilton.

Taiko – Union Steam Ship Co. of New Zealand Ltd (Wallem Shipmanagement), New Zealand; Mitsubishi HI, Nagasaki, 1984; 33,374 dwt, 174.86 m, 20 ta, 11,360 bhp Mitsubishi-Sulzer, 15 kn. (Authors' collection, above, & Tolerton, below)

Taiko, which had been launched as *Tara*, joined the coastal fleet in 1984, replacing *Erne* as the black oil carrier. Purpose-built for the trade and fitted with a bow thruster, she is illustrated (above) after her launch at Mitsubishi Heavy Industries, Nagasaki, and (below) in service.

Toanui – Seabird Ltd (Coastal Tankers) New Zealand; Mitsubishi HI, Nagasaki, 1987; 32,605 dwt, 182.40 m, 13 ta & 2 slop ta, 10,850 hp Mitsubishi-Sulzer, 14.5 kn. (Tolerton)

Also a product of Mitsubishi's Nagasaki yard, *Toanui* (above) had a relatively short career in New Zealand waters by the standards of her predecessors in the coastal fleet. Built in 1987 as *Australian Spirit*, she arrived in January 1996 and departed in 1999, being renamed *Lorenza* and then *Andoas*. A small legacy she left was in the revised funnel colours which she introduced with a pale blue-grey band between two white on the lower part of the traditional black funnel with silver fern emblem. *Kakariki* (below, pictured dressed on her maiden New Zealand port call at Lyttelton with a full cargo of petrol and aviation fuel from Geelong) was ordered in Poland and delivered in 1999. She has 18 cargo pumps (4x800 cu/m an hour, 8x550, and 6x300), and fuel consumption is 38 tn a day.

Kakariki – Penagree Ltd (Silver Fern Shipping), New Zealand; Stocznia Szczecinska, Szczecin, 1999; 46,724 dwt, 183 m, 20 ta & 2 slop ta, 12,019 hp Cegielski-Sulzer, 14.5 kn. (Tolerton)

Another view of the hard-working *Kakariki* (above), about to vanish into a fogbank off Banks Peninsula. She is designed to carry up to nine segregations of products as well as up to about 3000 tn of bitumen, and her Schilling rudder, highly skewed propeller, and bowthruster enable her to crab sideways or to turn 360 deg within her own length, giving her maneuverability not seen before in New Zealand waters for a ship of her size. The next addition to the coastal fleet was the chemical-products carrier *Torea* (below), built in South Korea in 2004 for South African owners and acquired in 2007. She had 12 cargo pumps each able to move 500 cu/m an hour. Fuel consumption was 36 tn a day.

Torea – Nyathi Ltd (Silver Fern Shipping), New Zealand; ShinA Shipbuilding, Tongyeong, 2004; 37,069 dwt, 175.90 m, 12 ta & 2 slop ta, 11,665 hp Doosan-B&W, 15 kn. (Tolerton)

Michael Pryce's first ship, *Hima* of 1957 (top), and views of *Hyria* of 1954 under construction at Lithgows (centre) and in service (above). He was serving on *Hyria* when she went to the shipbreakers at Kaohsiung in 1975. Left: Michael Pryce in his second year at sea as a deck apprentice on *Hinnites* at Stanlow in 1965. Boilersuits were worn far more often than uniforms. (Mike Pryce collection)

Tankerman

Captain Michael Pryce spent 23 years at sea with Shell, serving on 26 different ships. Here he looks at a well-remembered occasion for any seafarer — the first voyage — and life on product tankers of yesteryear and the last voyage of a tanker.

My First Product Tanker

After six months at Plymouth Navigation School, my first voyage beckoned in late 1964. The appointment letter from the company required me to join their tanker *Hima* at Berre. I have to confess that although I already knew much about tankers, Berre was a new one on me, and I needed an atlas to discover that this was in the south of France, west of Marseilles, where Shell had a small refinery on the inland lagoon of Etang de Berre.

Air travel to join ships was not yet in common use, especially for lowly deck apprentices, so after reporting to the prestigious Shell Centre in full uniform, the journey was by Golden Arrow train from London (Victoria) to Dover Marine, a channel crossing on British Railways ferry *Invicta* to Calais Maritime, by Wagon-Lits train to Paris (Lyon), thence to Marseilles (St. Charles), arriving at 4am, and being spirited away by the agent's runner to Martigues, Port de Bouc. After a day in a hotel, a launch took a colleague and I out to where *Hima* lay anchored off Port De Bouc, the general cargo port. In those days, the popular after-shave Old Spice was sold in glass bottles with a stopper top, and this was stowed in my suitcase. The stopper had come out during the journey, so when it was opened, all the contents of the suitcase stank of Old Spice. The smell of Old Spice still brings back memories of that day!

Hima, one of Shell's general purpose 18,000 dwt. tankers, was the only vessel of that class that was built by Odense Staalskibs at Odense, Denmark, before the shipbuilder moved to a larger shipyard at Lindo. Immediately east of Port de Bouc was the "supertanker" port of Lavera, where the giants (of that time) discharged crude oil from either the Persian Gulf or North Africa. (Eight years later, the new port of Fos was built further west, able to be used by laden VLCC's). Later that night *Hima* moved from the anchorage and berthed at Lavera to load avtur (aviation turbine fuel) or as it later became better-known, jet kerosene. After slowly part-loading via a single pipeline, two days later we sailed from Lavera and anchored-off, then later that day sailed through Port de Bouc via a canal and past a lifting-bridge into Etang de Berre and across to the refinery at Berre itself, on the far side of the lagoon, there to load petrol, kerosene, and diesel. Thence back through the canal to Lavera to complete loading with more petrol and diesel until full.

This pattern of multi-berth loadings seemed to be the norm, and certainly extended time in port. Most tanker berths were sited well away from populated areas in case a tanker blew up! This in the days before inert gas and double hulls. *Hima* was on Shell's "Medi" run, and discharged at Malta, Tobruk, Piraeus, loaded at Milazzo and La Spezia, and then discharged at Lisbon and Stanlow. Stanlow was the site of Shell's major refinery on the Manchester Ship Canal, and not the most exciting port to visit, although the nearby Beatles were all the rage at that time. After finishing discharge, the next voyage in ballast was to Shell's giant refinery at Willemstad, Curacao, to part-load more products, completing at Punta Cardon in Venezuela, all for discharge at Luanda and Ango-Ango (in the River Congo), then back in ballast to Curacao to load for Casablanca, Gibraltar, Algiers, Bone, Port de Bouc again, Naples, Malta, Piraeus, Larnaca, and then via the Suez Canal to Abadan. A very interesting itinerary, and for a ship enthusiast, lots of interesting old ships to observe!

The H class were cutting-edge technology when they were built in the mid-1950s, but were constructed before the era of automation and labour-saving devices, so needed quite large crews, as all deck valves (and there were a lot of them) were hand-operated, heavy natural fibre mooring ropes were heaved tight on steam winches, stoppered-off and turned-up on bitts. Lifting was by derricks, which needed a lifting wire on a steam winch, and rope guys to plumb it in the desired position, and all the cargo pump controls at the top of the aft pumproom were via extended-spindles, and hand-operated. Cargo work was all done manually, measuring ullages in cargo tanks every half an hour with linen measuring tapes with a wooden float on the end, topping-off with wooden ullage sticks, and taking samples with a brass sampling bottle to measure density and temperature. The paints in use were fairly conventional for the times, pre-epoxy coatings, and a constant battle was fought with rust.

The majority of tankers at that time were built with the navigation bridge/wheelhouse amidships (over the cargo tanks), where the deck officers were accommodated, with the engineers accommodated aft (near their beloved engines), and the deck and engine crew were accommodated in cabins within the hull aft. It was in 1972 before I sailed on my first 'all-aft' tanker. The dining saloon and galley were aft, so meal times meant a trek aft from amidships for the deck officers — which is why the flying-bridge had a couple of 'bus stops' fitted for shelter in bad weather.

Mechanical ventilation was fitted, as well as early air-conditioning units, whose performance varied! In cold weather, steam-heating was used to warm the air supplied to the accommodation, but getting the settings comfortable was always a challenge! The accommodation was comfortable, but nowhere near as luxurious as later "supertankers" had, but after a visit to some basic British tramps, we were usually very grateful to return to our lot. Steam turbine propulsion was the favoured main-engine at that time, having changed from the favoured diesels in the early 1950s – and before they reverted to favoured diesels after the 'Oil Shock' of 1973. Any tank-cleaning required involved use of Butterworth or Victor-Pyrate machines that were suspended in the tanks, and had hot water under high pressure squirted around the tank, while steam-driven portable fans attempted to keep tanks gas-free during this process. An 'Explosimeter' was used to check gas readings. This was manufactured by MSA (Mining Safety Appliances) — it was comforting to know that coal-mining technology was being used to keep us safe!

A comment is probably warranted about the catering arrangements of those times. No convenience foods had become normal then, and the cooks did a sterling job in producing fare that was plain but wholesome from raw materials. Milk in the pre-Long-life milk era was always a challenge, and was mainly provided by tins of sweet condensed milk, which usually meant that cups of tea did not need sugar added. Entertainment was provided by Walport, with early film projectors and reel-to-reel films, carried around in sturdy (and heavy) boxes, obviously designed to withstand six-inch shell blast in time of war! In tropical weather they would be shown onto a screen rigged on the flying bridge/catwalk aft of amidships, with the projector sited in the cargo office amidships. In bad weather the film would be shown in the aft saloon, with the projector safely secured by rope lashings. It was not unusual to experience a heavy roll and wonder if it would survive! It was usually the job of the deck apprentice to show the film and to change the reels when required, thereby gaining valuable experience in his chosen career?

In the 'before the internet' era, communications were not easy. In some parts of the world (Indian Ocean), the radio officer often needed to listen for company messages in the middle of the night (in Morse Code) in order to get through, and it was not unusual to find that a change of orders had been sent (but not received) 12 hours earlier, and that we were now steaming in the wrong direction! There were no ships bars at that time, and bottles of Oranjeboom beer would be consumed in cabins. Every Sunday, courtesy of the Dutch Royal family, one Oranjeboom bottle of beer was provided to everyone on board (our parent company was of course Royal Dutch-Shell). And it was much appreciated!

End of the line

Shell's 18,000 dwt steam tanker *Hyria* (12,131gt, built 1954, yard No.1074) was the first of four built by Lithgows at Port Glasgow, followed by *Hyala* (1081), *Hygromia* (1093) and *Hydatina* (1095).

They were welded ships, except that the hull plating was riveted to the frames. *Hyria* later commissioned the new Rock Ferry tanker cleaning berth in the Mersey in 1960, sited just upriver from Tranmere oil terminal, and intended to encourage tankers to utilise the various repair drydocks in the Mersey after tank cleaning and gas freeing at Rock Ferry. (This facility fell into disuse after 1983, although the derelict jetty structure still remains). In 1962, *Hyria*'s No. 11 centre oil tank was converted at Yokohama to carry bitumen, and two 100tn LPG tanks were fitted on her foredeck. *Hyria* then stayed in the Far East, trading out of the Pulau Bukom refinery, off Singapore. She became scheduled to operate the closest thing possible to a 'liner trade' for a tanker, making alternate voyages from Pulau Bukom to Shell's Nha Be installation (just downriver from Saigon) or to Shell's Kwun Tong installation at Hong Kong (adjacent to Kai Tak airport). In 1968, her No.7 centre oil tank was also converted to carry bitumen.

In April 1975, South Vietnam fell, or was liberated, (depending which "side" you supported), when *Hyria* was voyaging back to Singapore from Hong Kong, intending to load another cargo for Saigon. *Hyria* anchored in Singapore's Western Anchorage (off Pulau Bukom) on April 24, 1975, to "await orders". This was in the midst of the tanker slump caused by the massive increases in oil prices from 1973, and many tankers were laid up at anchorage, initially awaiting further employment, and later heading for Far Eastern scrapyards, especially if they were fuel-hungry steam turbine-powered ships. These included BP's *British Prestige* (27,049 gt/1962) and *British Power* (27,179 gt/1959). News was to hand of various other Shell tankers either being laid up in Brunei Bay or being scrapped.

By May 4, the date had come around for another voyage to Hong Kong, so *Hyria* berthed at Pulau Bukom to load oil and bitumen, then shifted to another berth to load LPG. *Hyria* sailed from Bukom on the afternoon of May 6. The small Vietnamese tanker *Truong Hai* was anchored in Eastern Anchorage. She was formerly the French Shell tanker *Cyprea*, looking similar to a flatiron collier, and designed to trade up the Mekong River under low bridges, which had arrived off Singapore with numerous Vietnamese refugees on board. On May 8 an abandoned lifeboat was encountered at sea, empty, but with a notice painted on the hull advising that occupants had been picked-up by a US Navy ship. At Hong Kong on May 11, *Hyria* berthed at Aplei Chow first to discharge oil to the power station, then moved around to Kwun Tong next day to discharge bitumen, LPG and residual cargo. *Hyria* sailed from Hong Kong on May 13 to return to Singapore, but later in the day, orders were changed to load at Miri (Sarawak) for Srirachi. Ominously, the ship was also instructed to "steam at 3 knots under charter speed like rest of fleet".

Next day, orders were changed again to load at Balikpapan for Kushima, Japan, and *Hyria* anchored in Balikpapan bay late on May 19, berthing two days later to load Minas waxy residues. Balikpapan was always an interesting place to visit, as the wreck of the stern and funnel of Eagle Oil's tanker *San Flaviano* was passed heading for the berth (*San Flaviano* was bombed and sunk during the Indonesian civil war in 1960). After completion of loading and sailing on May 22 for Kashima, orders were changed the next day to Yokohama and Kobe. While *Hyria* had been trading to Saigon, the company had deemed it politically expedient to have painted out the yellow shells on the funnel, so funnel was just red with a black top. Now that *Hyria* had rejoined the fleet, so to speak, it was decided that the shells should be replaced on the funnel. With no previous markings visible on the funnel, this was not an easy task, and although completed on May 29 it rather more resembled a squashed yellow cauliflower than the Pecten maximus shell intended! *Hyria* berthed at Yokohama on June 1 and cargo discharge commenced. The Kobe visit was cancelled, all cargo was discharged at Yokohama, and after anchoring for a few hours for engine repairs, the ship sailed on June 3. Miri light crude oil was loaded at Miri on June 13 and 14, for discharge at Shell's Tabangao refinery in the Philippines. It will be recalled that *Hyria* had her hull plates riveted to her frames. The very light cargo leaked slightly, so that when stopped on arrival awaiting a pilot, a bit of sheen was clearly visible around the ship. Sailing after discharge on June 18, orders were to return to Miri for another cargo, but in view of the perceived pollution risk, *Hyria* was ordered to Pulau Bukom to load a cargo for Townsville. While alongside at Bukom loading, the leaking rivets were plugged with Thistlebond, of which the ship carried ample stocks. A day after loading and sailing for Townsville, a crack in the bow plating flooded the lower peak flat, but this was plugged with Cordobond.

On June 27, news was received by radio that the ship was to be scrapped. "We confirm your vessel sold to Japanese buyers for delivery at Kaohsiung, Taiwan before 31/8/1975. Our intention is for you to proceed Kaohsiung after cleaning, etc, without further trading. Contract of sale requires all cargo tanks cleaned to hot work standards. No other spaces required to be cleaned. Kaohsiung authorities also strict regarding ballast cleanliness and amount of scale/sediment in tanks, therefore ensure that prior arrival Singapore, all tanks well-cleaned and lifted, leaving only slop tank to deal with in Singapore. To ensure satisfactory standards achieved, you are to obtain a gas free certificate in Singapore prior to departure. Following items to be landed in Singapore: a) Shell specimen, sponsor's gift and SES library, b) Unbroached stores for use on other vessels, c) Walport films and gear, d) Both inflatable liferafts with cradles, e) Any unbroached spare gear which is of use to other vessels, but only if new and high value. Sale includes LPG bottles and these also to be cleaned. Both steam capstans (from poop) complete to be landed in Singapore, earmarked for *Holospira*. Previous vessels sold Kaohsiung have been moored with anchors down and stern to berth, arrange tug assistance as required in view no capstans. Destroy all Admiralty documents by burning. Repack Admiralty Safe into box for landing."

After discharge at Townsville, the return voyage to Singapore was spent in preparing for her scrapping, including venting and gas-freeing both of the LPG tanks on deck. Arriving back at Singapore's Western Anchorage on July 17, 1975, even more ships were lying at anchor awaiting their fate. After berthing to discharge oil slops and a further period at anchor,the last voyage of *Hyria* started on July 22, at the stately speed of just under seven knots, "slow-steaming" indeed! *Hyria* anchored off Kaohsiung on August 1, and "berthed" in the scrap yards next day. However, "berthed" wasn't used in its normal sense. All ships being scrapped at Kaohsiung in those days dropped both anchors and were moored stern-to the shore. The local pilot merely sought out the berth of the local ship breaker who had purchased the ship, then lined her up, went astern, and "bashed" his way between other ships to get into place!

The surrounding scene was thoroughly depressing to a mariner, with about 30 ships in various stages of demolition, which in Kaohsiung started at the stern and worked forward. The bow of British India's liner *Nevasa* was still visible, and work was under way on *Ocean Monarch*. Shell's tankers *Hemiglypta* and *Isomeria* were already there. By the next day, the close proximity of Typhoon Nina had caused some local bad weather, and had blown all the ships down towards one end of the harbour, so all were lying hard alongside another ship, in the case of *Hyria*, wedged between the tankers *Olympic Valour* and *Courier* (ex-*Esso Durham*). The liner *Reina Del Mar* had arrived a few days before *Hyria*, and had been similarly affected, so it was quite easy to move from ship to ship to enable a visit to inspect that ship. All seemed quiet and gloomy, with all ventilation fans and lighting power turned off. All crew left *Hyria* on August 5, needing to climb ashore from the poop down a long wooden ladder that had been fortuitously found on board, as disembarkation by the planned launch alongside was impossible with a tanker tightly wedged on each side!

By one of those quirks of fate, the next ship to which I was appointed was *Holospira*. Stowed in a corner of the forward dry-cargo hold were found the steam capstans removed from the poop of *Hyria*, obviously un-needed and unwanted. Those items lay there until *Holospira* herself went for scrap. At the time of the mass scrappings taking place in 1975 and 1976, Shell's store in Singapore was overwhelmed with valuable spare parts for classes of tankers whose remaining lifespans were destined to be very short, but that was probably not certain at that time. *Holospira* was fitted with four steam turbine centrifugal cargo pumps. She also had five spare impellors for the above bolted to the bulkheads in her centre castle, and these also went to scrap with her.

Two views of *Hyria* in the log jam of ships awaiting demolition at Kaohsiung (top, Mike Pryce) and pictured on her last visit to Hong Kong, with a pair of LPG tanks on the foredeck and the Shell pecten absent from her funnel (left, Mike Pryce). The last H class ship to go to the breakers was *Halia* in 1985, reprieved mainly because she was used as a lightening tanker around the UK. The longest survivor among all the H, K, and A class tankers built for the Shell group was the Dutch-flag motorship *Acmaea* of 1959 (below, WSS/Keith Byass), which was sold to Troodos in 1986 as *Prophecy*, renamed *Dart* (1987) and *Delfi* (1988), and scrapped at Alang in 1995. Her life had been extended by service as a floating oil field storage tanker based off Thailand.

Sometimes the heat of Middle East refinery ports is almost missed by tankermen, like the crew of BP's *British Fulmar,* a 1959 Bird class completion from the Alexander Stephen & Sons shipyard, Glasgow, on this passage. She made two Baltic voyages, to Stockholm and to Turku, in one of the worst northern European winters in 1965-66. On the first to Stockholm she was icebound for 10 hours in the Landsort Channel before being freed by an icebreaker.

Ice Navigation

It's not all sunshine sailing on tankers. Ice navigation in the Baltic in winter was one of the special challenges BP product tanker crews took on. Captain David Barnes of Westport, New Zealand, who served with BP for 14 years from 1959 to 1973, recalls these winter voyages.

BP tankers were to be seen delivering products, both black and clean oil, throughout the year in the Baltic during the 1950s, 60s and 70s. There seemed to be about four or five vessels allocated to the UK–Europe–Scandinavian trades for varying periods as the trading situation warranted. None were specifically dedicated and the time 'on the coast' varied, but certainly for around four months at a time.

It was common for there to be an Extra Mate aboard due to the short trips and often lengthy stand-bys as many of the loading ports were located at ports with long river estuaries such as Hamburg or lengthy locking in, such as Antwerp, Swansea, and Grangemouth. The North Sea voyages seemed to consist of many foggy trips, significant weather, heavy traffic and fishing vessels of which the wooden, double-ended Danish boats were a nightmare. They were traditionally painted eggshell blue, blending perfectly with the prevalent mist and sea colour, making them very difficult to spot at the close quarter situations. Apart from the indistinct radar echo, in such conditions the only physical manifestation of their presence was the unmistakable steady 'tonk, tonk, tonk' exhaust of the single cylinder Bolinder diesel. Enough to raise the heart-beat of the master and the officer of the watch along with the hackles of their hair as they frantically tried to spot the demon. I well remember one such meeting and when eventually the vessel emerged into view it was going astern and with no one in the wheelhouse as both men were on deck sorting fish!

At the Skaw of Denmark we took aboard two Danish pilots to take us down through the Great Belt and into the Baltic proper. At these times there were still the designated tracks in the 'deep water' cleared of World War Two mines. For most of the year the tracks were buoyed but during the winter the buoys were lifted and navigation relied on positions fixed by traditional methods but mostly Decca, which all BP tankers were permanently fitted with. Other companies 'hired' theirs as and when needed, I believe. Once in the Baltic the Danish pilots were dropped at Trelleborg. Coming out of the Baltic on the way north we generally took a Swedish pilot at Trelleborg for the passage past Falsterbro, dropping him at Helsingborg, then we navigated the way out of the Kattegat and Skagerrak by ourselves up the Swedish coast which had deeper waters and supposedly no mines.

Going into the Baltic in winter during the ice season a Swedish ice pilot was taken at Trelleborg and he stayed aboard for the duration we were in the Baltic. The onset of ice is very quick most years. On one trip to Lulea, right at the top of the Gulf of Bothnia, we entered with just 'frazil ice' across the surface but three days later when we sailed the icebreakers had to break us free of the ice which was 100mm thick by that time. The temperatures had dropped drastically to around minus 25 Celsius and the water, being near fresh, readily froze.

On any trip where temperatures were expected to get near freezing, precautions were taken aboard. Steam was kept 'on deck' to power the windlass and winches, with each having a broad white band painted across their warping drums so we could ensure they were working. This also kept the all important steam line from freezing and ready for use. The salt water fire main had pressure on it with strategic valves open to allow water to keep flowing. A toilet was left running so that the sanitary tank on the monkey island did not freeze … this of course ensured a big icicle hanging over each side where the outflow was. Alongside this also ensured the loss of a 'chocolate box' or two as the build-up of ice on it ensured the breaking strain of the ropes holding it was exceeded. Generally these measures all worked pretty well. Shipping fresh water aboard was an art as it came aboard via the fire main and so all valves were opened at the start to clear any salt water and progressively shut as the water reached the freshwater tanks. When full, they were sequentially opened to ensure the line was drained so it would not freeze when the shore valve was shut.

The formation of ice on deck, mostly when in a loaded condition, was spectacular. With the ship loaded in winter conditions and a headwind and seas forward of the beam, the spray and water coming aboard rapidly froze. A few hours of this would ensure the build-up of ice on anything and everything it landed on. Flying bridge rails would quickly become coated and united to form a 'canal.' Valve wheels on deck would become huge mounds of ice. Rigging and stowed derricks breeding grounds for huge icicles…all very interesting for the first day, then it became a great trial clearing it to be able to work cargo. Those working on deck adopted some very innovative clothing for protection against conditions with any wind. Pyjamas over underclothes as first layers, thick shirts, as many socks as possible, two pullovers, a duffle coat topped with an oilskin to stop the wind and chill factor. The Michelin Man couldn't compete!

The ice pilot was invaluable of course as he kept abreast of the ice conditions and predicted position, the position of the ice packs dictating the course to be taken as they moved with the prevailing wind. The further north and later in the season, then the heavier the ice conditions and the more icebreaker assistance could be required, and while generally the Swedes had excellent command of the English language, the ability to converse fluently was all important.

One of the trickiest parts to navigate in the winter ice season was through the Aland Sea between the Baltic and the Gulf of Bothnia. This is comparatively shallow and so ice readily forms and accumulates here. There are also rocky shoals all about and should a ship become fast in the ice the danger of being taken aground by the moving ice packs was very real, needing quick assistance from the icebreakers. It's quite an experience being jammed in the ice at midnight on a clear and moonlit night…the ship surrounded by near silence and all about is white as far as the eye can see. That contrasted with the deafening rumble in the tanks when running lightship through the ice.

Mooring at a port where there was considerable ice brought a few problems as the space between ship and berth was blocked with ice broken up prior to the vessel's arrival by the tugs. Actually getting alongside was not always possible due to this factor, in which case a line was run out fore and aft with a couple of springs and the ship left to just sit there while the ice refroze to hold her. The pipelines were dragged out over the ice to be hauled aboard and connected. Clean oil ship discharges were more or less problem free. On the other hand discharging fuel oils, more often than not heavy fuel oil, was a different kettle of fish. Although most lines ashore were insulated, the plug of oil left in the line had solidified and the heating needed time to liquefy the oil. Sometimes the 'shore side' were lax and we had to apply 120psi for a few hours to extrude the slug and get to a state where we could pump properly. Not that we were ones to complain… Swedish ports were good fun and often had a nurses' home to provide visitors to a party aboard. Any delay was welcome.

Apart from the usual ports of Norrköping, Stockholm, Gävle, Sundsvall, and Luleå, there were quite a few off the beaten track particularly for black oil ships, mostly in small towns hidden away with a pulp mill to supply. The clean oil ships had some 'secret' discharge locations where the ship tied up alongside a cliff and aviation turbine gasoline was pumped into Swedish Air Force storage caverns deep in the hillsides.

On arrival at the final discharge port after a trip in heavy ice the wind and waterline around the forward part of the ship was usually like polished stainless steel. Summer was a different story … Norrkoping and the archipelago all the way up to Stockholm with the myriads of islands, baches all over the place with Swedish flags proudly fluttering at the mast, the sun and its worshippers to be gazed upon as we passed. Many was the time the motor lifeboat was dropped and loaded up for a Banyan Party ashore!

The BP tankers *British Merlin* (foreground), *British Reliance* and *British Fame* off Stockholm in November 1968; below, two views of *British Beech* of 1964, berthed at Lulea after completing discharge with David Barnes in the foreground (below, left) and sailing from the same port (below, right). (photos, David Barnes collection)

Two deck views of the 13,829 dwt *British Corporal* of 1954 (right and below) showing the accumulation of ice in a winter Baltic passage, and a view of the same ship flogging into heavy seas (top) in the 1968 Baltic winter. (David Barnes collection)

British Merlin (16,346 dwt/1962) with her bow frames scoured and exposed after a winter voyage in Baltic ice (above). Not only BP's ships braved the Baltic in winter. Below is an unusual view of Shell's Dutch-flag motor tanker *Acmaea* of 1959, the last ship of the famed H, K, and A class series to go to the breakers, iced up at, probably, a Baltic port. (David Barnes collection, above; Mike Pryce collection, below)

Shell tankers in Vietnam during the war: Above left and left: Two views of *Amastra* of 1958, after being sunk in shallow water by a limpet mine at Nha Trang in April 1967. She was salvaged and repaired, and sailed on for Shell until 1985 when she was the last of the A class to be disposed of from the UK fleet. (Mike Pryce collection)

Top right: *Hanetia* at Vung Ro (Mike Pryce).

Below: *Haminea* at anchor waiting to discharge at Da Nang in December 1969. (V.H. Young and L.A. Sawyer)

Tankers at War

Vietnam

The US involvement in the Vietnam War has been the subject of numerous films and books, writes Mike Pryce. From July 1965 the war began to require large numbers of ships, and many were reactivated from Reserve Fleet sites, were reconditioned in the USA, and sailed with military cargoes to hastily-developed port facilities in South Vietnam. Commercial ships were also taken on charter, with a large number, naturally, being US-owned. Fuel supplies were also needed for the large number of aircraft, helicopters, patrol craft and road vehicles used in the conflict. Termed POL by the military (petroleum, oil, lubricants), their mission was to supply avgas, JP4, mogas and diesel fuel to the combat and support forces. In the main, these fuels were supplied by civilian companies under contract to the military, and such supply contracts were held by Shell, Caltex and Esso. Singapore, lying only a few days steaming from South Vietnam, was the obvious closest main supply source, and it was from there that several interesting voyages were made to South Vietnam in 1968 and 1969.

Shell's *Hanetia* (12,189 gt/1957) sailed from Shell's refinery at Pulau Bukom, off Singapore, on 10 June 1968, after loading a full cargo, plus fenders, for the Vietnam Coast run. An extra precaution before sailing was for everybody on board to receive a plague vaccination, as this had broken out in several areas in Vietnam. Some 770 miles later, *Hanetia* anchored in Cam Ranh Bay on 13 June for cargo measurement, sampling, and awaiting orders. Other ships in port were the tankers *Prairie Grove* (15,462/44), *Amtank* (14,151/45) and the cargo ships *Beauregard* (9016/45), *Clarksburg Victory* (7607/45) and *Lakewood Victory* (7607/43). Most interesting were five T2 tankers, moored alongside each other, with sterns to the shore, in use as Army floating electric power supply ships —*Memphis, Lone Jack, French Creek, Logans Fort,* and *Cumberland.*

During the night, patrol boats criss-crossed the harbour, dropping concussion grenades to deter any swimmers from planting limpet mines on the hulls of ships. Sometimes, if dropped too close, it was not unknown for all the electrical breakers to be tripped "off the board", plunging the ship into darkness. On June 15 the US Navy tanker *Piscataqua* berthed alongside *Hanetia* and loaded 550 tonnes of avgas, after which *Hanetia* sailed in the early evening, leaving astern the sight of tracers being fired from one side of the bay, and flares continually drifting down over the airstrip.

A mere 45 miles north, *Hanetia* reached Nha Trang, but as entry of shipping at night was banned, the ship slow-steamed off the port and entered at dawn on June 16, berthing with the stern moored to buoys, and both anchors down, with cargo discharge via a submarine pipeline. The troopship *Upshur* (12,660 gt/1952) and cargo ship *Luen Tung* (2940/43) were in port, and also two more T2s in use as Army power ships, *Kennebago* and *Tamalpais.* Discharge was slow because of the low pressure required, and because of the requirement to pump seawater in between grades, and it took almost 24 hours to discharge 1938 tonnes of avgas, mogas and diesel, sailing in mid-afternoon for another short 55-mile voyage north to Vung Ro, where *Hanetia* anchored at sunset on 17 June as her sister ship *Haminella* (12189/57) sailed.

Vung Ro lay between Cap Varella peninsula and the mainland, and was quite small, and most evenings spectacular firepower displays took place as tracers and shells were fired from the peninsula, past the stern, onto hills on the mainland to deter night attacks. The mooring buoys were out of position, preventing discharge, so the ship spent a couple of days awaiting new orders. On the evening of June19 *Hanetia* sailed another 65 miles further north to Qui Nhon, arriving after dark, and again slow-steaming outside until morning, anchoring on June 20. Other ships in port were *City of Alma* (6065 gt/1945), *Overseas Rose* (7882/44), *Metapan* (6573/47), *Earlham Victory* (7607/45), *Green Mountain State* (7641/45), and *Steel Seafarer* (7698/45).

Haminella was in the anchorage, discharging into the US Navy T2 *Mission Santa Ynez,* and all fuel brought from overseas was discharged at Qui Nhon by lightening operations. On June 21 *Mission Santa Ynez* berthed alongside *Hanetia,* and was filled to capacity, after which the T2 sailed into the port, berthed out of sight around a corner and discharged it all ashore. Next alongside *Hanetia* was another Navy tanker, *Rincon,* followed again by *Mission Santa Ynez,* and it was June 25 before a total of 15,700 tonnes of JP4, mogas, and diesel had all been discharged into them. These old Navy tankers were maintained in immaculate condition. While at anchor discharging into them, several other ships had arrived, the cargo ships *Robin Gray* (7702 gt/1943), *Cape Sandiego* (6690/44), *Sixaola* (5026/47), and the troopship *Geiger* (12660/43) had sailed. With all cargo now discharged, *Hanetia* sailed south to Singapore, passing another sister ship *Khasiella* (12119/56) heading north for the same ports. At Singapore *Hanetia* bunkered and stored, then sailed for the Persian Gulf for a cargo.

Financial incentive to go into the "war zone" came in the form of double pay for all the time spent in Vietnamese waters, with a minimum five-day payment. This payment was not tax-free, however! Back from the Gulf, *Hanetia* discharged cargo at Pulau Bukom, then backloaded for the Vietnamese coast again, sailing on 29 July, with heavy rain and gales encountered on the voyage north, anchoring off Qui Nhon on August 1. The cargo ships *Cibao* (5026 gt/1947), *Everlucky* (9172/46), *Foh Kong* (1908/44), *Hannibal Victory* (7607/45), and *Sgt. Truman Kimbro* (AK 254) were in port.

Some cargo was discharged to *Rincon* again, and then *Hanetia* sailed on August 2 for Vung Ro, where *Overseas Dinny* (6153/43) and *Navajo Victory* (7609/44) lay anchored. At Vung Ro, the buoys had been repositioned, and after mooring to four buoys, *Hanetia* discharged 6422 tonnes via two submarine pipelines, sailing on August 5 back to Qui Nhon, where another 10,6980 tonnes was discharged into *Mission Santa Ynez* again, two new arrivals since the previous visit being *Pacific Reliance* (9337/51) and *Steel Apprentice* (7730/44). With all cargo discharged, *Hanetia* sailed on August 7, 1968, back to Singapore, and then carried several cargoes in the South China Sea area.

The Vietnam coast was reckoned to be the "safest" option if trading to Vietnam, where the biggest danger was from Viet Cong limpet mines. *Amastra* (12273/58) had been mined aft and sunk in shallow water at Nha Trang in this manner in April 1967 and *Helisoma* suffered bow damage from the same cause at Nha Trang in December 1968.

The next voyage of *Hanetia* to Vietnam was to Saigon, or more correctly, to Nha Be, the oil port 10 miles downriver from Saigon, where Shell had operated a terminal since the turn of the century. The voyage to Nha Be was reckoned more of a "hot spot" ever since *Haustrum* (12090/54) was hit in the wheelhouse by rocket fire in 1967. For protection in the wheelhouse/bridge whilst transiting the river, steel helmets were supplied to protect the head, flak jackets by Wilkinson Sword protected the body (I had thought that they only made razor blades), and a form of armoured Y-fronts (also by Wilkinson Sword) protected the nether regions. This equipment was very heavy, and the effect of wearing this in an un-air-conditioned wheelhouse in the tropics, with sandbags outside the wheelhouse doors preventing any breeze from entering, can well be imagined.

Hanetia anchored off Cap St. Jacques, at the entrance to the river, on October 9, 1968, where the cargo ships *Benjamin Chew* (7246 gt/1942), *Baylor Victory* (7607/45), *Pelican State* (7613/44), *Belgium Victory* (7608/44), and *Clarksburg Victory* (7607/45) already lay. The 40-mile river passage was made next day, passing up the strategically-important Long Tau River without incident. The river ran through the Rung Sat, a delta area produced by several small rivers and laced with myriad canals, a swamp of nipa palm and mangrove. To prevent mining of ships in the channel, in co-ordination with rocket attacks, the banks of the Long Tau had been drastically defoliated by use of Agent Orange. Berthing at Nha Be on October 10, the tanker *Eleftheroupolis* (13,066/58) lay on the adjacent berth, mined the previous night but not too badly damaged.

While discharging, the tanker *Texaco Bombay* (13899/45) arrived, and the cargo ship *Charlotte*

Appendix:
Shell movements

This list of movements of Shell's product tankers fleet at the end of April 1969 gives a picture of typical voyaging at that time:

British flag fleet:

Acavus (s) sailed Naples 27/4, arrived Tripoli (Lebanon) 29/4 to discharge part cargo. Then Benghazi (due 30/4) to complete discharge, then Curacao via Gibraltar for bunkers.

Achatina (s) sailed Curacao 28/4 with fuel oil for Searsport (Maine, US), diverted Bucksport (Maine) 30/4 due 3/5. Then to Curacao for orders.

Alinda (s) arrived Gothenburg 28/4 to load white oils for discharge Stockholm and Norrköping. Due 2/5 and 4/5.

Aluco (s) sailed Bandar Mahshahr with white oils 22/4 for part discharge Gan Island (due 29/4), then Colombo and Singapore.

Amastra (m) sailed Isle of Grain 20/4 in ballast clean for Curacao.

Amoria (m) sailed Singapore 26/4 with white oils for Noumea (due 8/5), Vatia, Apia, Papeete, then to Bukom.

Anadara (s) sailed Pernis 27/4 with white oils for Stanlow (due 29/4), then to sail to Hamburg to load white oils for Dingle.

Arianta (s) arrived Bangkok 26/4 to discharge white oils, sailed in ballast 27/4 to Bukom to load white oils for Bangkok.

Asprella (s) arrived Botlek, Rotterdam, 29/4 to discharge part cargo chemicals, then Swansea-Stanlow (due 2/5 and 4/5), then repairs for seven days and proceed Curacao.

Aulica (s) sailed Freetown 21/4 in ballast for Curacao, diverted Cardon 28/4, diverted Curacao 30/4. Due 1/5 to load fuel oil for Searsport and South Brewer, then to load Cardon-Puerto Miranda for Buenos Aires.

Axina (s) arrived Miri 29/4 to load white oils for Bukom, due 2/5. Then to load Pladju and Balikpapan for Yokkaichi.

Hadra (s) sailed Curacao 9/4 with part cargo luboils for Cardon, arrived Cardon 10/4 to complete loading, sailed for Singapore 10/4 via Durban for bunkers to discharge part cargo, then to Saigon and Djakarta.

Hadriania (s) sailed Gothenburg 28/4 with four grades of white oils for discharge Ornskoldsvik (due 1/5) and Hudiksvall, then to proceed via Kiel Canal to Thames to load white oils for Hamble and Stanlow, then to reload white oils for Old Kilpatrick and Ardrossan, then to Curacao for orders.

Halia (s) at Qui Nhon from Bukom to discharge white oils, sailed 29/4 in ballast for Miri (due 1/5) to load white oils for Bukom.

Haminea (s) arrived 26/4 at Bukom from Saigon in ballast, sailed 27/4 with four grades of white oils for discharge Bangkok, then to sail Singapore for orders.

Haminella (s) arrived Jurong 14/4 from Bukom to drydock.

Hanetia (s) arrived Bukom 24/4 from Bandar Mahshahr with white oils, then to reload with white oils for Saigon, then Singapore for orders.

Harpula (s) Arrived Sao Luiz 29/4 from Fortaliza to discharge part cargo of white oils and sailed 29/4 for Belem to complete discharge.

Hastula (s) arrived Penang 28/4 from Port Dickson to discharge black oils, sailed 29/4 for Singapore to load black oils for Hong Kong.

Hatasia (s) arrived Bukom 29/4 from Miri to discharge three grades of black oils, then to reload black oils at Bukom for discharge Tanjong Pagar, then to load black oils at Bukom for Yokohama-Shimonoseki-Kokure.

Haustellum (s) arrived Lagos 20/4 for station tanker duties.

Haustrum (s) arrived Curacao 29/4 from Genoa to load 10 grades of luboils, then to sail for Rotterdam (due 15/5) to discharge and reload part cargoes, then to Thames for discharge, then ballast clean to US Gulf to load luboils for Curacao.

Heldia (s) arrived Singapore 22/4 from Cardon to discharge aviation fuel, sailed 24/4 in ballast for Mina al Ahmadi, but likely to be diverted to Bandar Mahshahr to load naphtha for Yokkaichi.

Helisoma (s) sailed from Cardon 24/4 with gasoline and naphtha for Thames (due 6/5) and Stanlow (9/5), then to Bremerhaven to dry dock.

Hemicardium (s) sailed Yokkaichi 23/4 in ballast clean for Curacao via Balboa.

Hemidonax (s) arrived Tabangao 27/4 to load black oils for Bukom, then to load fuel for Kobe and Shimonoseki.

Hemifusis (s) arrived Capetown from Saigon in ballast 18/4 to bunker, sailed 19/4 for Houston.

Hemiglypta (s) on Australian coastal trade, under Australian flag.

Hemimactra (s) arrived Curacao 27/4 to discharge part cargo white oils, then load avtur (aviation turbine fuel) for discharge Honolulu (due 13/5).

Hemiplecta (s) sailed from Kobe 29/4 with balance of fuel cargo for discharge Yokohama (due 30/4), then to sail for Pladju (due 9/5) and Sambu to load black oils for Japan.

Hemisinus (s) sailed from Cardon 29/4 with avtur for Sewaren (New Jersey) (due 4/5).

Hemitrochus (s) arrived Fremantle 27/4 to discharge part cargo lube oils, sailed 28/4 for Adelaide to discharge further part cargo (due 1/5), then to sail Melbourne, Geelong, Sydney, Brisbane, Wellington to complete discharge, reload at Geelong with part cargo luboils for Wellington, then ballast to Curacao.

Hima (s) arrived Yokohama 29/4 to load part cargo kerosene, sailed 30/4 for Yokkaichi to complete discharge white oils ex-Bukom and load part cargo kerosene for Bukom.

Hindsia (s) sailed from Sydney 30/4 with part cargo black oils for Geelong, then to sail in ballast for Pladju and Sambu to load fuel oil for Bukom.

Hinea (s) sailed from Curacao 18/4 with part cargo und and carbon black feedstock for Puerto Miranda, arrived 19/4 to complete loading with TJP crude, sailed 20/4 for Swansea to discharge part cargo, then to Stanlow to complete, then to Cardiff to dry dock.

Hinnites (s) arrived Yokkaichi 29/4 to discharge full cargo naphtha and load part cargo lube oil, then to Woodlands (due 11/5) to discharge, then ballast to Persian Gulf to load white oils for the UK-Continent.

Holospira (s) arrived Pladju 26/4, sailed 29/4 with part cargo fuel oil for Sambu, then to reload part cargo Minas waxy residue, then to sail to Bukom to complete with fuel for Yokohama.

Horomya (s) sailed from Bukom 25/4 with white oils for Suva (due 9/5), Vuda, Geelong, and Wellington.

Humilaria (s) arrived 27/4 western anchorage, Singapore, shifted to Jurong 28/4 for drydocking.

Hyala (s) sailed from Pauillac 29/4 in ballast dirty for Thameshaven (due 1/5) to load full cargo waxy distillate after tank cleaning, for Rotterdam Pernis.

Hydatina (s) sailed from Bombay 27/4 with white oils for Madras (due 1/5), then to Calcutta to complete discharge.

Hygromia (s) arrived Bukom 23/4 to discharge part cargo white oils and reload further part cargo for Tabangao, then complete loading for Hong Kong. Then to sail in ballast to Miri to load white oils for Bukom.

Hyria (s) sailed from Bukom 28/4 with black oils for Saigon (due 29/4), then to return Bukom to load black oils for Hong Kong.

Dutch flag fleet:

Abida (m) arrived Douala 25/4 to complete discharge white oils, sailed for Curacao 26/4 in ballast. Acila (m) arrived Bukom 29/3 to complete discharge lube oils, sailed 30/3 for Curacao in bal last via Cape of Good Hope.

Acmaea (m) sailed from Bukom 26/4 with white oils for discharge Cam Ranh Bay (due 28/4), then to Pladju in ballast.

Acteon (m) arrived Purfleet 30/4 to discharge white oils, then to Donges (due 3/5) to load white oils for Stanlow, then reload for Avonmouth-Thames-Rotterdam.

Arca (s) after drydocking at Flushing sailed 18/4 for Curacao, diverted Point Fortin 23/4, diverted Curacao 28/4, and due 30/4 to load white oils for Anchorage (due 19/5), then return Curacao in ballast.

Atys (s) sailed from Mina al Ahmadi 28/4 with white oils for Bukom (due 8/5).

Camitia (m) arrived Stanlow 28/4 to discharge part cargo lube oils and reload for discharge Barton, then Rotterdam to load part cargo luboils for discharge Lisbon, then to Curacao intended to load for Stanlow and Barton.

Cinulia (m) sailed from Cardon 11/4 with luboils for Durban (due 2/5) and Ango Ango (Congo), then Curacao in ballast clean.

Crania (m) sailed from Cardon 29/4 with luboils for Rotterdam (due 14/5), Stanlow, and Barton.

Kabylia (s) sailed from Durban 13/4 in ballast for Curacao, diverted 24/4 to Point Fortin (due 29/4) to load part cargo of LDF for Curacao, then to load white oils at Curacao and Cardon for Thames-Stanlow.

Kalydon (s) sailed from Point Fortin 25/4 with white oils for Sewaren (due 1/5) and Baltimore, then to Cardon in ballast to load white oils for Sewaren.

Kara (s) sailed from Bombay 29/4 with white oils for Madras (due 3/5) and Calcutta, then to Arabian Gulf in ballast.

Katelysia (s) arrived Sambu 21/4 to load fuel oil, sailed 23/4 to Bukom to discharge, sailed 26/4 with black oils for Sorong and New Caledonia, then to return Bukom.

Kelletia (s) sailed from Rotterdam 19/4 in ballast for Curacao, diverted Cardon 29/4 to load white oils for Rotterdam.

Kenia (s) sailed from Danang 26/4 in ballast for Bukom (due 29/4).

Kermia (s) sailed Durban 27/4 after bunkering, with white oils for Bukom (due 11/5), then to reload white oils for Saigon.

Khasiella (s) sailed from Ince 21/4 in ballast dirty for Curacao, diverted Cardon 2/5 to load black oils for Houston (due 9/5).

Kopionella (s) arrived Miri 21/4 to load black oils for Bukom and Port Dickson, then to backload black oils at Port Dickson for Bukom.

Koratia (s) after discharging white oils sailed from Bukom 28/4 with white oils for Saigon (due 30/4), then to Miri in ballast clean to load white oils for Bukom, and back load white oils for Bangkok.

Korenia (te) arrived Cam Ranh Bay 9/4 to discharge part cargo white oils and sailed 9/4 for Nha T rang to complete discharge.

Korovina (s) sailed from Bahrain 24/4 for East London with white oils, diverted Durban (due 5/5), then to East London to complete discharge, then to sail to Durban in ballast clean to load white oils for Port Elizabeth.

Kosicia (s) arrived Curacao 28/4 to load white oils for Bukom (due about 1/6).

Kossmatella (te) sailed from Capetown 25/4 after bunkering en route Aruba to Bukom with white oils.

Krebsia (s) arrived Eastham 16/4 to discharge full cargo of white oils, sailed for Curacao 17/4 to load white oils for Kingston-Clifton Pier-St George.

Kryptos (s) sailed from Cardon 24/4 for Montreal (due 1/5) with white oils, then to Curacao in ballast clean, then scheduled to load white oils at Cardon and Aruba for Singapore.

Kylix (s) arrived Curacao 27/4 to load white oils for Lobito, Ango Ango, Lagos, and Ascension Island.

Demise managed fleet:

Alkmaar (s) arrived Capetown 29/4 from Durban to discharge part cargo white oils then reload white oils, then to Walvis Bay to discharge (due 3/5), then Curacao in ballast clean.

Ameland (s) arrived Thameshaven 29/4 from Stanlow with parcel of medium cycle oil, then to sail for Rotterdam in ballast clean to load parcel laws for discharge Jarrow, then to Rotterdam in ballast clean.

Cerinthus (s) arrived 29/4 at Cardon from Curacao with parcel und and to load parcel of slack wax , then to sail for Puerto Miranda to complete with TJP crude, all for discharge at Stanlow (due 14/5).

Clymene (s) arrived at Mina al Ahmadi 24/4 from Dar Es Salaam in ballast clean, and sailed 25/4 with gas oil for Bukom.

Dorestad (m) sailed from Piraeus 29/4 for Tunis to discharge balance of cargo of white oils, then in ballast clean for Curacao.

Eastgate (s) arrived Bukom 17/4 from Bandar Mahshahr to discharge balance cargo of white oils, sailed for Woodlands 19/4 with new part cargo of white oils, sailed for Port Moresby 20/4 to discharge part cargo, then to Brisbane and Sydney to discharge the balance.

Forthfield (s) sailed from Eastham 29/4 in ballast clean for Amsterdam to load white oils for Copenhagen (due 5/5), then to Rotterdam in ballast clean to load white oils for Thameshaven.

Kaap Horn (s) arrived Anchorage (Alaska) 21/4 to discharge white oils and sailed 22/4 for Curacao via Panama Canal in ballast clean (due 9/5).

Keizerswaard (m) sailed from Lavera 23/4 in ballast, to load at Cardon and Curacao for Thameshaven and Stanlow.

Koningswaard (m) arrived Thameshaven 29/4 to load black oils for Llandarcy (due 2/5) and Ardrossan, then to Rotterdam in ballast dirty to load black oils for Casablanca, Moni, and Larnaca.

Maloja (s) sailed from Hammerfest 19/4 in ballast clean for Cardon and Curacao to load white oils for Singapore.

Mantua (s) started ascending River Seine 29/4 and berthed Petit Couronne 29/4 to load white oils for Curacao.

Purmerend (s) arrived Capetown 26/4 to bunker en route to Rotterdam with white oils.

Schelpwijk (s) after discharging white oils sailed from Bangkok 24/4 for Singapore to bunker, then ballast clean to Bandar Mahshahr to load white oils for Mauritius and Dar Es Salaam.

Stonegate (m) sailed from Mukalla 30/4 for Aden to complete discharge of part cargo of white oils, then to Assab to load part cargo of white oils for Massawa, Port Sudan, and Mombassa.

Thirlby (m) sailed from Hamburg 29/4 with white oils for Teesport, then scheduled to ballast clean to Rotterdam to load white oils for Hamble and Stanlow, then ballast clean to Hamburg for white oils for Teesport.

Vlieland (s) sailed from Curacao 26/4 with white oils for Wilmington and Harbour Island via Panama Canal, then scheduled ballast clean to Acajutla to load white oils for Cutuco.

Westertoren (s) sailed from Los Angeles (Wilmington refinery) 19/4 in ballast clean to load white oils at Curacao and Kingston for discharge Clifton Pier, Freeport, and St Georges.

Two well-known Shell tankers of this era, *Halia* (above, Chris Howell collection) and *Hemiplecta* at Hobart (below, D E Kirby/R A Priest collection). *Halia* was the last H class to go to the breakers.

Addendum

Silver Gwen – Marina Lolite Shipping Ltd (Sinokor Maritime Co), Panama; Hyundai Mipo, Ulsan, 2014; 49,746 dwt, 183.06 m, 12 ta & 3 slop ta, 10,469 bhp Hyundai-MAN-B&W, 14kn. (Anton de Krieger)

Royal Dutch Shell, the biggest charterer of products tankers, is revitalising its fleet via Project Silver (see also P149), a programme in which 50 MR vessels are being built for long term charter to Shell by Hyundai Mipo. The chemical-products tanker *Silver Gwen* of 2014 (above) was the 14th completion in this programme, and one of 34 being built for Sinokor of Seoul, whose funnel colours she displays. The 25th completion was the *Silver Dubai* in 2015 (below).

Silver Dubai – Silver No.20 SA, Panama; Hyundai Mipo, Ulsan, 2015; 49,780 dwt, 183 m. (Anton de Krieger)

British Mariner – Hai Kuo Shipping 1511 Ltd (BP Shipping Ltd), Isle of Man (UK); Hyundai Mipo, Ulsan, 2016; 45,999 dwt, 183.06 m, 9160 kw MAN, 15 kn. (BP)

British Navigator – BP Shipping (mgr), Isle of Man (UK); Hyundai Mipo, Ulsan, 2016; 45,999 dwt, 183 m, 9160 kw MAN, 15 kn. (BP)

BP has also been renewing its fleet at Hyundai Mipo, announcing a US$573m order for 14 MR tankers in 2013. In contrast to Shell's Project Silver charter programme, the BP vessels are for its own account and British-flagged, registered in Douglas. The first, the 45,999 dwt *British Mariner* and *British Navigator*, were delivered early in 2016 (see also P175). The new Mariner class ships update the similar sized Virtue class of 12 ships, also from Hyundai Mipo, delivered in 2004-05, like the *British Chivalry* (below).

British Chivalry – Kelso Ltd (BP Shipping), UK (Isle of Man); Hyundai Mipo, Ulsan, 2005; 46,803 dwt, 183.22 m, 12 ta & 2 slop ta, 12,870 hp Hyundai-B&W, 14.6 kn. (Tolerton)

Stolt Emerald – Stolt Emerald BV (Stolt Tankers BV), Cayman Islands (UK); Daewoo Shipbuilding, Geoje, 1986; 38,719 dwt, 176.80 m, 54 ta, 12,480 hp Hyundai-B&W, 15kn. (Anton de Krieger)

While many product tankers now are classified as "chemical/products" carriers, several companies have long specialised in the carriage of chemicals, and among the foremost for more than four decades has been Stolt Tankers, with a world-wide network of parcel tanker services. Among the sophisticated vessels in its deepsea fleet have been parcel tankers of the *Stolt Emerald* class of 1986 (above) and the *Stolt Vestland* of 1992 (below) and her sisters. Designed for "drug store trading" often carrying small volumes of expensive specialty chemicals, the *Stolt Emerald* had 54 segregated tanks (two of them for slops) plus four deck tanks, with the centre tanks and deck tanks made of stainless steel. The *Stolt Vestland* had 41 segregated tanks and two deck tanks, and a travelling gantry crane for hose handling.

Stolt Vestland -- Stolt Vestland BV (Stolt Tankers BV), Cayman Islands (UK); Kvaerner Kleven, Floro (aft section) & KK, Forde (fwd), 1992; 31,434 dwt, 174.70 m, 39 ta & 2 slop ta, 3.5 tn cr, 12,472 hp Bryansk-B&W, 15.5kn. (Anton de Krieger)

Stolt Creativity – Stolt Creativity BV (Stolt Tankers BV), Cayman Islands (UK); Danyard A/S, Frederikshavn, 1997; 37,271 dwt, 176.75 m, 42 ta & 4 dk ta, 5 tn cr, 4 x Wartsila diesel electric engines & 1 Leroy-Somer elec motor, 18,172 hp, 16.2 kn. (Anton de Krieger)

More modern additions have been the *Stolt Creativity* (1997) types (above) and *Stolt Perseverance* (2001) types (below). Both classes have diesel electric machinery. The *Stolt Creativity* class also introduced a membrane nitrogen inert gas system, and the cargo tanks and bunker tanks were enclosed in a double hull. The *Stolt Perseverance* was double-hulled. All four Stolt tankers illustrated have been registered in George Town, Cayman Islands.

Stolt Perseverance – Stolt Perseverance BV (Stolt Tankers BV), Cayman Islands (UK); ACH Construction, Le Havre (hull), & Brodogradiliste, Pula (completion), 2001; 37,059 dwt, 176.70 m, 46 ta & 2 slop ta, 4 x Wartsila DE engines & 1 elec motor, 18,172 hp. (Anton de Krieger)

Lancing – R/A Hildegaard (Lundqvist Rederierna), Finland; Blythswood SB, Glasgow, 1950; 18,752 dwt, 166.02 m, 27 ta, 5600 bhp Rowan, 12 kn. (World Ship Society/Keith Byass)

A 1950 completion from Blythswood Shipbuilding, Glasgow, the 18,752 dwt *Lancing* (above) saw service under two Scandinavian flags, Norway's and Finland's, without change of name. She was built for Melsom & Melsom, whose previous *Lancing*, sunk during World War Two, had been the first whaling factory ship with a stern ramp. The 1950 *Lancing* was sold to prominent Aland Islands owners Lundqvists in 1960 and registered at Mariehamn, and is seen in her Lundqvist days in this photograph. She was scrapped at Gijon in 1978. Representative of a later tanker generation in Finnish ownership was *Kotka Rose* of 1982 (below), which was registered in the small port of Kotka and presumably locally-owned. She was built in Japan as the Greek *Ocean Runner* but taken over by the Finns after completion, and traded under eight names before going to Chittagong in 2009.

Kotka Rose – Kansallisrahoitus Oy, Finland; Kanda Zosensho, Kawajiri, 1982; 29,999 dwt, 172.02, 21 ta, 11,200 bhp Hitachi-B&W, 14.5 kn. (Tolerton)

Acknowledgements and Bibliography

The authors are grateful to many individuals who helped in the preparation of this book, particularly Captain David Barnes, master maritime photographers Trevor Jones (Durban), Anton de Krieger (Vlaardingen), Russell Priest (Melbourne), Chris Howell (Invercargill), and the late Keith Byass (Bingley) who generously made so many images from their collections available, Bill Thomson editor of *The Motor Ship,* David Whiteside of the World Ship Society, John Clarkson (Ships in Focus), Mason Tolerton, Everard Tolerton, Rosemary Radujko, Geoff Churchman of transpressnz.com, Warren Nelson general manager of Silver Fern Shipping, Andy Copping, and the staff of Christchurch City Libraries.

World Ship Society *Marine News,* New Zealand Ship & Marine Society *New Zealand Marine News,* Hawkes Bay NZS&MS *Leading Lights, Lloyd's List, The Motor Ship, Sea Breezes, Ships Monthly, Mobil Compass, The Log* (Nautical Association of Australia), *Clansman* (British & Commonwealth house magazine),*Ropner Record,* Silver Line Newsletter, *Ocean* (Ocean group magazine).

Appleyard, HS *Turnbull, Scott & Co;* Bakke Jr, Dag *In Storm and Calm Seas: Helmer Staubo & Co;* Bock, Bruno & Klaus *Soviet Bloc Merchant Ships;* Bramsen, Bo *A Hundred Years of Dannebrog;* Burnett, Robin *Water under the Keel;* Crowdy, Michael *The Eagle Tankers* (WSS); Dear, Ian *The Ropner Story;* Dick, HW & Kentwell, SA *Sold East;* Dick, HW & Kentwell, SA *Beancaker to Boxboat;* Dunn, Laurence *The World's Tankers;* Farquhar, Ian *Howard Smith Shipping;* Faulkner, Alan *Tankers Knottingley;* Foustanos, Georgios *Tankers Built for Greeks, 1948-65 & 1966-90;* Gray, Leonard *H Hogarth & Sons Ltd;* Gray, Leonard *The Ropner Fleet 1874-1974* (WSS); Greenman, David *Jane's Merchant Ships 1999-2000;* Greenway, Ambrose *Soviet Merchant Ships;* Grey, Michael *Chemical/Parcel Tankers;* Grey, Michael & Scott, *Robert Product Tankers and their Market Role; Half a Century of Silver Line;* Harlaftis, Gelina *A History of Greek-Owned Shipping;* Harvey, WJ & Solly, RJ *BP Tankers, A Group Fleet History;* Harvey, WJ *Hadley;* Heaton, PM *Jack Billmeir Merchant Shipowner;* Hooke, Norman *Modern Shipping Disasters 1963-1987;* Hornby, Ove 'With Constant Care...' *A P Moller: Shipowner;* Howarth, Stephen *Sea Shell; Huntings of Newcastle Upon Tyne; Japan Ship Exporters' Association Shipbuilding and Marine Engineering in Japan* (various vols); Jenkins, J Geraint *Evan Thomas Radcliffe;* Johannesen, Ole Stig *Maerskbadene II;* Johannesen, Ole Stig *Maerskfladen 1976-90;* Johannesen, Ole Stig *The Torm Ships;* Jordan, Roger *The World's Merchant Fleets 1939;* Kolltveit, Bard & Pedersen, Bjorn *Wilh. Wilhelmsen 150 Years;* Lingwood, John *Significant Ships* (various vols); Lingwood, John & O'Donoghue, Kevin *The Trades Increase* (WSS); Lloyd's Register *Register of Ships* (various vols); Long, Anne & Russell *A Shipping Venture, Turnbull Scott & Co 1872-1972;* Malpas, P. *Fairplay World Shipping Directory;* Messenger, Commander Nick *Ships taken up from Trade Report for the UK Ministry of Defence Directorate of Naval Operations & Trade;* Middlemiss, NL *The Anglo-Saxon/Shell Tankers;* Middlemiss, NL *The British Tankers;* Mostert, Noel *Supership;* Musk, George *Canadian Pacific;* Newton, John *A Century of Tankers;* Perry, FW & Laxon, WA *Nourse Line;* Rabson, Stephen & O'Donoghue, Kevin *P&O A Fleet History;* Rabson, Stephen *P&O in the Falklands;* Sampson, Anthony T*he Seven Sisters;* Sawyer, LA & Mitchell, WH *Empire Ships of World War II;* Sawyer, LA & Mitchell, WH *Sailing Ship to Supertanker, The 100 Year Story of British Esso;* Sawyer, LA & Mitchell, WH *Tankers;* Sawyer, LA & Mitchell, WH *Victory Ships and Tankers;* Sedgwick, Stanley *London & Overseas Freighters PLC* (WSS); *Shipwatch Directory;* Solly, Ray *Athel Line, A Fleet History;* Stewart, IG *BP Tanker Company;* Wouters, Wim *Shell Tankers Van Koninklijke Afkomst;* Villar, Roger *Merchant Ships at War, the Falklands Experience;* Vodena-Mitsiou, Maria *10,000 Years of Greek Shipping Vol.2.*

Websites : Auke Visser's Esso, Mobil, & T2; Historical RFA; Helder Line; Tyne Built Ships; Wikipedia.

Chevron Pacific – Chevron Transport Corp (Chevron Shipping Co), Liberia; Mitsubishi HI, Kobe, 1983; 34,950 dwt, 179 m, 19 ta, 11,400 bhp Mitsubishi-Sulzer, 15 kn. (Tolerton)

Mitsubishi's Kobe yard completed a distinctive class of six tankers in 1981-83 for Chevron. Liberian-flagged, they were 34,950dwt, 15kn ships with, an innovation at that time, enclosed lifeboats. The first of the class was *Carla A. Hills* of 1981, followed by *Alden W. Clausen* and *George H. Weyerhaeuser* (1981), *Samuel H. Armacost,* below, and *Kenneth T. Derr* (both 1982), and *Chevron Pacific* (1983), above. The latter, later renamed *Raymond E. Galvin* in 1996, had 19 tanks instead of the 15 of the others in this class. All had four cargo pumps moving 4600 tn an hour.

Samuel H. Armacost – Chevron Transport Corp, Liberia; Mitsubishi HI, Kobe, 1982; 34,950 dwt, 179.23 m, 15 ta, 11,400 bhp Mitsubishi-Sulzer, 15 kn. (Tolerton)

Index of ship names

A familiar sight in New Zealand ports and on her seaways: The coastal tanker *Kakariki* discharging at dusk in Dunedin (above) and steaming through Cook Strait (below) on her way north to pick up another cargo of products and bitumen at Marsden Point. (see also page 214). Photos: Andy Copping

New Zealand's newest coastal tanker, the 50,300 dwt *Matuku*, arrived at Marsden Point on June 30, 2016 to enter service for Silver Fern Shipping. She is pictured above berthing on her second visit to Marsden Point (photo Andy Copping) and below at the Seaview terminal on her first Wellington visit (photo V. H. Young/L.A.Sawyer).

The introduction of *Matuku* made *Torea* superfluous, and she sailed from Marsden Point on July 7, re-registered in Singapore, and bound for Botany Bay and then Bulwer Island refinery, Brisbane, with a cargo of heavy fuel oil before ballasting to Singapore for redelivery to Unicorn Shipping management. See also page 196.

Andy Copping photo.